THE
SONORAN
DESERT

PHOTOGRAPHS BY JACK W. DYKINGA

TEXT BY CHARLES BOWDEN

THE
SONORAN
DESERT

HARRY N. ABRAMS, INC.

PUBLISHERS

A NOTE FROM THE PHOTOGRAPHER:

The plants fill any frame taken in this desert, but this book is not a guide to their names. Stone, too, fills the dry world, but the deep lore of the rocks will be found elsewhere. I am in love with the place. Though its borders are often hazy to our science, its presence is often unmistakable to those of us who call it home.

–JACK DYKINGA

Front cover: BRITTLEBUSH, OCOTILLO AND A LONE SAGUARO CACTUS. CARNEGIE PEAK, SIERRA PINACATE, PINACATE PROTECTED ZONE.

Back cover: MORNING CLOUDS AT HORSESHOE BEND OF THE SALT RIVER. SALT RIVER CANYON WILDERNESS, TONTO NATIONAL FOREST.

Page 2: SANTA CATALINA MOUNTAINS, CORONADO NATIONAL FOREST

Editor: Robert Morton
Designer: Robert McKee

Library of Congress Cataloging-in-Publication Data
Bowden, Charles.
The Sonoran Desert: Arizona, California, and Mexico /
photographs by Jack W. Dykinga; text by Charles Bowden.
p. cm.
ISBN 0–8109–2669–5 (pbk.)
1. Natural history—Sonoran Desert. 2. Desert ecology—Sonoran Desert.
3. Natural history—Sonoran Desert—Pictorial works.
4. Desert ecology—Sonoran Desert—Pictorial works.
5. Sonoran Desert. 6. Sonoran Desert—Pictorial works. I. Dykinga, Jack W. II. Title.
QH104.5.S58B68 1992
508.791'7—dc20
92–7223

CONTENTS

*Oftentimes we Americans feel contempt for empty
land and its animals—things we hardly know and
cannot dominate. We fear the unknown.*

Ed Abbey taught us not to fear.

JACK DYKINGA

*For Margaret, Cami, and Peter,
whose love has endured the best and worst of times.*

J.D.

*For Jesse.
This is your country, boy.*

CHARLES BOWDEN

ACKNOWLEDGMENTS

Susan Anderson, The Nature Conservancy, Latin American Division; Tom and
Susan Bean; Bill and Terry Bendt; Dave Brown; Bill Broyles; Tony Burgess, The Desert
Laboratory, United States Geological Survey; Dan Campbell, Arizona Nature
Conservancy; Tom Dollar; Bunny Fontana; Julian Hayden; Charles T. Mason, Jr.;
Sandy Smith; Ray Turner, The Desert Laboratory, U.S.G.S.; Rebecca Van Devender,
University of Arizona Herbarium; Andrew Wigg, Bureau of Land Management;
Joe Wojcich, Tempe Camera Repair.

Special thanks to the University of Arizona's Southwest Center and its director,
Joseph C. Wilder; to the editorial staff of Arizona Highways *magazine*
and its publisher, Hugh Harelson; to Phil and Ardus Hyde for shared camps and
ideas; and to Janice Emily Bowers, of The Desert Laboratory, U.S.G.S. for countless
hours of photographic taxonomy. To Bob Morton and Christine Liotta whose integrity and commitment
to excellence made a difficult job easy.

Finally, to Ginger Harmon, whose generous support made this book possible.

Thanks,

J.D.

ASK SIMPLE QUESTIONS, BECAUSE THE ANSWERS TO
COMPLICATED QUESTIONS PROBABLY WILL BE TOO COMPLICATED
TO TEST AND, EVEN WORSE, TOO FASCINATING TO GIVE UP.

Alfred W. Crosby, Ecological Imperialism: The Biological
Expansion of Europe, 900–1900,
Cambridge University Press, New York, 1986

MARK TWAIN WAS RIGHT. BETTER THE SAVAGE WASTELAND
WITH EVE THAN PARADISE WITHOUT HER.

Edward Abbey, Down the River,
E. P. Dutton, New York, 1982

Six Part Invention
by Charles Bowden

ONE

They sweep down from the foothills and the higher plains, from the country of the oaks and grassland. They move as a family, helping each other, communicating with each other, the bodies flowing over the land, a culture sharing the chore of training up the young. They are interlopers and where their mark stabs into the soil a kind of fear spreads, a vibration rolling out from their path. They do not like the coyotes and these are killed or driven off. The lions are competition and so the cats are forced to the higher, rockier ground. They like the night, and they answer its blackness with sound. Few living things ever see them, that is their custom.

The deserts they sometimes visit, making flying raids as a group, sweeping down from their homes looking for the deer, the rabbit, the occasional other creature. And then they depart. Here, where the rains do not come often and water is scarce, the heat is intense, the trees few, the plants thorned, here they are interlopers, visitors who do not choose to raise their young in such a place, transients who know their limits and stay within them. When we finally come into this country, we call them wolves and we slay them.

There is a group of them this day in March 1942 nestled on a mountainside in the Huachucas near the Mexican border. Sometime in the winter, the male mated with female and now they feed and protect the pups. The forest above them is a relict of the Pleistocene, from that time about ten thousand years ago when the world here changed yet again and the rains ceased to visit as often. A man comes named Bill Casto. He works for the government of men in an organization called Predator and Rodent Control and his group operates at will everywhere in the West. They take the bear, the lion, the coyote and they kill them. But most of all they want the wolf. Casto is the man for this work.

In 1909 a rancher in Colorado had sent for him and he came and killed wolves and got $50 per animal and a .35-caliber Winchester lever-action rifle as a bonus. In 1911 he was ranching in the Blue River country below Alpine, Arizona, when wolves, he later said, wiped him out financially. Since then he has killed wolves and other takers of flesh for a living.

He traps the male living on the slopes of the Huachucas and kills him. He finds the den and clubs the pups to death. The bitch flees and streaks south down into Mexico. That is the last time a pair of Mexican wolves (Canis lupus baileyi) ever breed in Arizona. They become extinct on the land throughout the entire region. A great silence falls like lead on the night and a howling that had raked the dark hours here for thousands of years ceased.

I am hiding on a roof under the desert sun. Last night I sat in the darkness on a nearby hillside. At first the coyotes cried out and their voices sang from the various surrounding slopes. And then suddenly a larger sound lifted up into the blackness and the howl of a wolf rang out under the stars. Now I look down carefully at the two animals who made that sound. I am at the Arizona-Sonora Desert Museum near Tucson, and in a small pen defined by cyclone fencing sit two Mexican wolves. They are part of twenty-nine such animals in the United States, all part of a captive breeding program aimed at reintroducing them to the land. Ten more live in cages in Mexico, and experts think a few handfuls remain wild and free up in the Sierra Madre.[1]

The animals below me are not really of the desert. But then neither am I. Where my kind live, the desert is absent or kept at bay. When we first came to this ground, we huddled by rivers and springs. Now we punch deep holes into the ground and suck up the buried water or we dig huge trenches and propel it uphill for hundreds of miles. We build houses and inside these dwellings the temperature is not like the white heat outside. We use machines to comfort us. We grow grass. The desert begins wherever we end, and we look at it with fear and hope and, for reasons we cannot quite explain, with longing. Like the wolves awaiting the outcome of our plans in their pen, we are interlopers in this place and we have yet to face this fact. We have yet to know what they know. But this has long been so.

We do not know why we like deserts. But we know from the records left in our books and our language that this feeling is recent in our minds and hearts, and that our acts constantly belie our words and feelings. For Americans, this change in attitude probably first occurred in the 1890s among a select and cursed few. For Mexicans, this change may never have occurred, their attitude may have been a constant that avoids the prickly question of like and dislike and simply takes things as they are. This time the desert is a dry slab knifed by mountains, a hot pan spreading across southern Arizona, deep into Sonora, embracing Baja and probing fitfully and with caution into the polluted air of California. The mountains run roughly northwest by southeast with valleys of soil between them that have been ground down by the hand of time from their flanks. There have been accidents and this is the result. They say that between 650 million and 250 million years ago shallow seas ebbed and flowed across southern Arizona. No one really remembers. There was a great continent called Pangaea and forces ripped it apart 225 million years ago and the land throbbed with volcanoes, earthquakes, and dances of the earth's crust. The troubles continued. Maybe 35 or 25 million years ago the ground exploded and thousands of cubic miles of rock roared up from the depths. This energy declined and then 15 million years ago the crust of the desert began to pull apart and rows of mountains separated by valleys filled with eroded soil gave the land its new look, one the men of science called Basin and Range. In the eastern portions of this desert, the peaks have pine, spruce, Douglas fir—all these survivors of a kind of climatic holocaust that occurred about ten thousand years ago. The valleys themselves seem to deny the word desert at first, at least by our normal standards. There are too many trees—mesquite, ironwood, palo verde—and the ground is teeming with too many plants. Huge cacti— saguaro, hecho, organ-pipe, cardón—tower over everything else, the largest cacti on the face of the earth. But the rains do not lie and this desert drinks from eleven inches of rain a year down to two or three—and in some years none at all.

The life witnessed here has almost always come from elsewhere. Many are extensions of the tropics—the cacti, for example—and in this place they must outwit a world so dry the air seems like sand in the mouth. The cacti store moisture in their flesh until the rains

BARREL CACTUS AND TEDDY BEAR CHOLLA AMONG GRANITE STREAM STONES. DIABLITO CANYON, PARQUE NACIONAL SIERRA SAN PEDRO MARTIR

come again. The trees, they drive deep into the earth. Living mesquite roots have been found at over 150 feet below the surface. In summer, the soil temperatures can soar to 160 degrees or more, and little or nothing stirs in the midday heat. The coyote beds down until the cool hours near dusk. The birds go quiet. The rattlesnakes are not out and about; the ground heat would kill them in minutes. Some animals—the kangaroo rat and possibly the Sonoran pronghorn—never even drink but are able to find moisture in their foods. Most simply evade. The Gila monster, that poisonous symbol of this desert, spends ninety-eight percent of its time underground. Essentially, it does not live in the Sonoran Desert, it merely surfaces at those fine moments when the temperatures are mild and the living is pleasant.

This baked but sacred ground is the place often scorned or feared, the place where early priests found Satan everywhere, and where earlier Americans found many, many gods. For thousands of years it has been a theater for invaders—invading plants, invading animals, invading Homo sapiens with various baggages of beliefs. It is one of the world's many stages and like any stage it tolerates performances but is resistant to any permanent occupation by the players. Here the cast is always killed—that is part of the play. This is my desert. It prompts no clear agreement on maps, but is called the Sonoran Desert with various academic quibbles about its exact borders. But it truly exists and anyone can visit it. It is not always a pleasant place. But it is very, very beautiful and few who feel its lips on their mouths can ever leave it. Any more than they can permanently remain truly in it. That is the lesson of the wolves we might consider as we tend to them in the cages we have wrought. We keep brushing up against this point, over and over, century after century.

We live in a truly unique moment. We are probably the first generation since prehistoric times to see and feel the world as a whole. We are certainly the first generation since time began for our species to have the capacity to destroy the living fabric of life that sustains our species. And we are certainly destroying it. The deserts, though grievously damaged, have been largely spared our appetites until very recently. We did not fully understand how we could kill them and eat them. Now we know how and this knowledge comes to us at the very instant in our history when we begin to have the first glimmerings of understanding the desert and other ecosystems. While deserts are hardly the richest of the earth's biological systems, they are the most visually striking to our dulled senses. Is it an accident that a totally industrialized, drugged, and urban generation of Americans has flocked to the image of the desert as a source of renewal? The question facing us, all of us, is whether with our new knowledge and our large demands on the planet we can stay our hands and leave the deserts alone, leave one last sanctuary for the other life forms that sustain the fabric we call earth, leave one last place where silence is the normal sound?

Homo sapiens now eat heavily of the earth's real food, the amount of energy captured by plants through sunlight. Recent estimates peg our consumption at forty percent of all the production of photosynthesis either through direct consumption or through disturbance. There are somewhere between five and thirty million species on earth (we will never know, we have identified only 1.4 million). Though but one species, we devour forty percent of the food on the table. Optimists warn this rate cannot persist without a crash that will *diminish or wipe out human numbers. Pessimists predict a crash within a hundred years that may destroy the entire system itself—not just people, but all living things as we know them.[2]*

We are at the crucial moment in the commission of a crime. Our hand is on the knife, the knife is at the victim's throat. We are trained to kill. We are trained to turn the earth to account, to use it, market it, make money off it. To take it for granted. Logically, we will never be able to reverse this part of our culture in enough time to stop that knife in our hand. But that is the task at hand—to cease this act of violence. Everything we love, and everything we think we are, will be gone, will cease to be, unless we manage to change. We will either produce descendants who think a cactus, a rat, an insect, and a snake are as important as human beings, or we will not leave descendants. In the short run it pays to do as we have always done, lest we have less treasure with which to comfort ourselves in the dark and lonely nights. In the short run it might theoretically pay a hungry human being to eat its own liver, as one scientist has put it. But in a slightly longer run such a diet would be fatal.[3]

The deserts, those scorned regions where Christ was tempted by Satan, those parched sectors that our ancestors loathed, are next on our menu. And the only thing that may save them is the idea of the desert that we are just beginning to grasp and entertain—the idea that deserts are places we cannot have, cannot conquer, cannot turn to account.

It is an idea that lurks in our records. Once I opened a book and this dead priest started talking. He has been dead for 218 years. It is night and the light of the electric bulb pours down the page. Outside a monsoon wind shakes the mesquite trees as the leathery whispers of the dead priest float across the room.

He lives in the Alsace-Lorraine, a place of snow in winter, green trees in summer, but Father Johann Jakob Baegert, S. J., writes in his fifty-third year of another place halfway around the world, Baja California. He had been cast out of the New World by order of the Spanish king and now he fattens in the Germany of his youth. For seventeen years he has toiled about two-thirds of the way down the peninsula at the Mission San Luis Gonzaga, and his memories are often ash in his mouth and bitterness on the page. He strains to remember: it is 1751 and he must cross over to his new assignment. The hollow log is about thirty feet long and four feet wide. For two and a half days of rowing and sailing he crosses the Sea of Cortez and hits Baja.

I pause and wonder what must have been the terror of spending two and a half days in a hollow log on such a notoriously treacherous sea. We tend to see the earlier padres as eccentric figures, men wearing long frocks and mentally trapped in some textbook memory we have of the Middle Ages. It is a jolt, a useful one, to realize they were often brave and, at times, heroes. This priest survives his hard passage across the waters and spends almost twenty years in Baja building a stone church at his isolated mission. I decide to go there and so I do.

I walk down toward the wash, a green cut through the hard surrounding desert. Water runs along the surface, palms lean across a small pool. A dozen people dressed in clean cotton clothes, a pig snuffling around their feet. They stare down at the ground as I walk

PURPLE MAT (*Nama demissum*) FLOWERS AMONG JAWBONES OF A DESERT BIGHORN SHEEP. SIERRA PINACATE, PINACATE PROTECTED ZONE

through. The church is made of small rocks, the pews few and hard. In Baegert's day, there were most likely no pews at all and the Indian congregation undoubtedly stood for the mass, but still everything seems very close to the time more than two centuries ago when the father must have left it.

I can hear him complaining: "Everything concerning California is of such little importance that it is hardly worth the trouble to take a pen and write about it. Of poor shrubs, useless thorn bushes and bare rocks, of piles of stone and sand without water or wood, of a handful of people who, besides their physical shape and ability to think, have nothing to distinguish them from animals, what shall or what can I report? . . .

"It would be far more profitable for any man to receive a village of one hundred peasants or to be mayor of a small market town than to be Grand Duke or Hospodar of California."

He dips his quill in the inkwell, pauses ever so briefly, and more words flood the sheet of paper: "Nothing is so common in California as rocks and thorns, nothing so rare as moisture, wood, and cool shade. It is not necessary to be afraid of drowning in California, but it is easy to die of thirst. . . . Just as the California soil appears to be pure rock, the sky above it seems to be made of steel and bronze."

Baegert has second thoughts. How can a man spend seventeen years tending the children of God and not find something good and valuable and worth his while? The pen races down the page. The natives of Baja California?

They are much happier than people in Europe, even happier than the rich and comfortable. The native sleeps better on hard ground than a rich man does on his feather bed. "In all his life," the priest insists, "the California native never has, or learns, anything to worry or distress him or to destroy his joy in life and make death desirable. Furthermore, there is no one, neither inside California, nor outside, to plague or persecute him, or to throw a lawsuit around his neck; no hail or army to lay waste his land, no fire or lightning to burn his barn or his farm. There is no envy, no jealousy, no defamation or slander to injure him. He has no fear of losing his property, no ambition to increase it. There is no moneylender to collect debts, no official to demand tribute, duties, head, road, and a hundred other kinds of taxes. There is no wife to hang more on her body than income warrants, no husband who spends on gambling or wine the money which should feed and clothe his family. There is no worry about the education of his children, no daughter to marry off, no depraved son to bring disgrace and ruin upon his house. In one word, in California and among the native Californians there is no 'mine and thine.' . . .

"Hardly one among them has a gray hair."

The sun is very hot while I listen to this dead priest's voice in the wind, a thin voice now telling me these things with the force of a reed trying to beat against a rock. I know I am the only person in this village at the moment who can hear Father Baegert. This is an affliction that has dogged me all my days. For me the past is never really dead and gone. It can be forgotten, like an old debt, but like a debt it still has demands on the present whether we recognize them or not. This was also true for Father Baegert in his day when he came to what his culture called a New World, and presented what he believed to be the true faith to a group of human beings who stood before him with thousands of years of the desert housed in their flesh, their bones, and their minds. We can know the past or not know the past but we cannot escape its cold hands or dry breath. The men of the modern village tell me a priest comes to the old church once each year at Easter. I nod at this information and think of the centuries of baptisms and burials, the Latin chanted by a string of human beings who cannot remember the beginning of such acts of devotion in this place or imagine the end of them.

Baegert himself, he spends every day at his job for seventeen years and the work, he whispers to me, is not easy. After five years Father Baegert decides he has figured the Indian out. He sits in his hut on the southern end of Baja and writes bitterly to his brother in Europe: "Last year a brand new set of mass vestments was given to me as a present by a benefactor and everything accompanying it, including the altar cloth, all silver cloth, with the bases trimmed in red with golden fringes and plenty of lace three fingers wide. . . . I used the vestments for the first time on Saint Aloysius day [June 21] and the Indians looked and admired it as little as if it was only made of camel's hair and the golden laces and fringes were only woolen strings."

He decides that they refuse "to admire anything."

Father Johann Jakob Baegert, S. J., cannot pry the natives from the devil and time after time they listen to the words of sorcerers. After seventeen years in Baja California—years full of sacrifice when he baked during the day, sweated at night, years full of scorpions swarming over the walls of his small room, and Indians stealing whatever was not tied down, after years of giving his all for God's glory in this hard land—he must face some unpleasant and almost unbearable facts. "Some of my parishioners," he notes with disgust, "believed themselves to be descendants of a bird, others of a stone which was lying not far from my house, while others dreamed of something different along the same lines. Each dream in turn was more absurd and more foolish than the other."

They would never prepare for confession and this drove Father Baegert crazy at times. And if they prepared, they immediately returned to their sinful ways. Once the priest confronted a woman who had failed to do her penance, simply saying several rosaries. Why, he asks, did you not do this simple thing?

She answers, "Because I was eating."

In frustration, Father Baegert asks another woman what she had done before he arrived and created this mission offering the saving grace of Christ.

"Nothing," she replied.

He is tired but something occurs to Father Baegert, something that must go in a letter to his brother in Europe. "Something else comes into my mind," he writes, "which was told to me and which I believe. When one described Hell to the Indians with all the fire and devils, they said, that is just what we desire and are looking for."

Father Baegert and I are trapped in this odd moment when almost two and a half centuries crumble like the walls of a crypt and we suddenly can confront each other and hear each other's words. It is September 11, 1752, and still very warm in Baja California. It is a September day at the end of the twentieth century and still very warm in Baja California. We, Father Baegert and I, are interlopers here, now, then, always. This is a very fine thing to be because it means we may always have a place we can go to when we need to comfort that empty part of our beings.

SPINES AT THE TOP OF A CARDÓN CACTUS (*Pachycereus pringlei*). PUERTO LOBOS, SONORA, MEXICO

There are so many deserts for us, since our minds cannot rest, and we often fabricate them. Sometimes I live in a very sad desert, one that almost breaks my spirit. Seven or eight centuries ago people set 800 stones in a circle and tried to catch a star. Or so some of us think. They call the place Zodiac Ridge and soon it will be gone.

Zodiac Ridge is a place I keep coming back to because it makes me face what I am doing to myself and my native ground. Some people think the rocks outline a simple ceremonial center—others find bewitching alignments that track key planets, powerful constellations. I come here because I can hear the whispers of the dead people, the vanished human beings who knew this hard desert world. I stare down into the circle and find a window—the face bouncing back at me is brown, the eyes almond and vacant, the lips barely moving. I strain forward to catch the slightest sound. I am hungry for a message. Tucson has gone from 150,000 to over 600,000 souls in thirty years and this stampede of people into the desert has shaken me. I crave the sure hand of the past on the shoulder, want to feel the dry, bony fingers steadying me as I lurch toward the roar of the Sunbelt.

Somewhere out in America hundreds of thousands of people are thinking of moving toward this circle of rocks. Every banker, developer, demographer tells me this fact. The new people will come for the warm days, clear skies, big mountains—and they will come here for Zodiac Ridge. This hot, thirsty earth sells because it promises what money really can't buy: a physical link to distant drums and gods. You park your car, walk a few yards, the rumble of rock 'n' roll from the radio still ringing in your ears, and suddenly you are in a circle of stones and your lips say Zodiac Ridge. The Southwest is a place where even the deaf can still hear the thin, dry voices of the past.

Of course, these voices are dying acre by acre, just as the game beats away before the black tongues of our pavement. The new call of the wild is the full-throttle growl of earthmoving machinery. The bulldozer is a far stronger drug than the abandoned shrines and sacred points of earlier Americans. The bulldozer seems stronger than all of us. Already a bulldozer has accidently crossed the ridge, bumbling on its way toward the future. People, people just like me, will finish this spot. We cannot seem to stop ourselves, we are too ravenous for the West of our dreams.

The new sacred circle will be a concrete and steel ring of subdivisions.

Sometimes I worry it won't be enough.

For any of us.

Sometimes I know.

But there are other times, and they fill me with life. I cannot remain depressed about change and destruction when the desert keeps reminding that it has, can, and will persevere. I have become, by chance, part of a web of life that tells me with every rock, thorn, and flicker of a lizard across the burning ground that it can go the distance and I can be a part of this unfolding without apparent end. I think of a tale once told me. About thirty years ago a friend of mine was in the Pinacate, a volcanic wilderness in northwestern Sonora close by the American border. No one can live in the Pinacate, there is no living water. My friend looked down and saw the track of a *wolf. He photographed it with a ruler by the imprint and decades later the track was verified. What could a lobo be doing here? Ah, an interloper. But then so am I in this place.*

There are many such instances that give me comfort. It is winter and the cold rains sometimes come. I am with a friend and we are walking and before we end, we will have walked two hundred miles. And it will not be enough. The rock here is black and tongues of lava splay out from the peaks across the bare ground. There are deep craters, and bighorn sheep, and antelope, and a silence past my understanding. We sleep by Elegante Crater, walk up past Suvuuk to Tinaja Emelia, climb the peaks, descend, and cut across the canyons of rock. Indian camps are here and there, the cook fires cold for a hundred years, a thousand years, ten thousand years. I can still remember the days and the nights. An owl spooked from a small ironwood tree at noon and racing terrified across the naked land before its enemies—every other bird on earth—can see it. The courtship flight of a hummingbird right before me as I sprawl on the ground, the tiny animal inscribing huge ellipses against the blue sky. The night pulling across my face like velvet, the coyotes singing, and then the dark hours with stars poking at my eyes. This is one of the few places on earth where I have heard the stars, a low humming as they slowly swing from horizon to horizon.

Eventually we come to a hole in the rock where the occasional rains collect and, until the air sucks them dry, such holes constitute the floor under much of the life here. This tinaja, tank, *is called* cuervo, raven, *and lies down a cliff in the rock-lined wash below. I make my bed in a sleeping circle, an arc of stones possibly thousands of years old and thrown up by other people to break the cold of the wind. I do not think now; that activity has ceased days ago. And if I dream, such things do not ride with me at the break of day. I float with memory, but everything is present, at this moment.*

Once I spent a day with an old man in the desert just to the north of me, a short brown figure squinting at me just on the other side of that line that divides nations but not a desert. The man is somewhere in his seventies and makes camp with his ninety-year-old sister twenty miles from the failing mining town of Ajo. Between his door and Yuma, Arizona, a hundred and twenty miles away, no man lives. His name is Chico Shunie and he is a Sand Papago, the end of the line of a certain stamp of desert people.

He has no car, no electricity, no running water. His home is a shack made from scavenged sheets of metal and cardboard. He speaks no English and hosts few visitors. He lives in a dead village, he and his sister the last residents it is ever likely to have. His people were the last true nomads to survive in the lower forty-eight states. Now federal park lands, a wildlife refuge, and military gunnery ranges have taken their ground and they as a people have all but melted away into the towns bordering their ancient homeland. Chico Shunie has not melted away. He lives within a federal wildlife refuge: the government chooses to ignore his presence rather than tangle with his possible legal rights. Around his ramada and his shacks the ground is plucked clean of vegetation, so that, he explains, he can see the rattlesnakes coming.

Inside his head is the lost world. Each season means different plants on the desert floor. The game beats away, the game gathers, all this movement is in his head. He knows where the tinajas, *the small, cisternlike holes in rock where rainwater collects and lingers for a*

BEYOND A DRY LAKE RISES PICACHO DEL DIABLO. PARQUE NACIONAL SIERRA SAN PEDRO MARTIR

while, hide among the jagged flanks of the mountains. He goes not to doctors. He announces that the desert is his medicine chest and in it he finds the right leaf, seed, root, and gum for whatever ails him.

But, he says, very little ails him. He has quit the drinking. Drinking, he says softly, that is what killed the other Indians. Now he plans to live forever. He cooks over mesquite gathered from the desert. He has no radio, no television; he cannot read or write. He has no way to cool the air except to rest beneath his ramada. He sits there day after day and floats his mind across the idea of the desert.

We get up from our chairs and walk down the wash. His sister remains behind—she is blind. He is going to show me the burying ground. The old man moves nimbly. His shoes are cast offs that do not fit his feet, his legs are short, stumpy and yet powerful. We move through the mesquite and up a slope and find a jumble of tilting crosses on a hillside. Many of the graves have collapsed into themselves. He points out his family—father, mother, grandparents, and on and on. He plucks a yellow flower and deeply inhales the scent. There is a promise of rain in the air. The flower's pollen leaves a yellow stain across his fingers.

A young Indian girl translates for me. Chico Shunie makes a leering comment to her and she laughs. He plans to live forever.

I have stopped thinking, as I explained, and things just flow across my life as I walk my two hundred miles across the desert. This goes on day after day. There are colors from flowers—the orange of globemallow, the yellow of brittlebush—and there is the play of light. I consider not leaving. I see the outline of a big animal at my feet, an intaglio created of stone by other people at an earlier time.

There is a cave where an Indian god lives. I leave an offering. Other matters occur.

I get out, I must. I am the interloper. What I find and want, I can only have if I leave. I assume this is some kind of sacred duty because it feels that way. But what matters is that suddenly I know I am not of this place and do not belong here and that there is no study of ecology or botany, no bath in some thing called nature that will alter this fact. There is no process of modifying my behavior, no simple environmental checklist that will render me into something that fits into this baked ground. I can only limit the damage I cause, savor the moments, and life is nothing but moments or it is nothing at all.

When I look back and see my footprints I am spooked by them. When I look up during the day and see the jet trail of a commercial airliner etch across the blue, I wish to shoot it down. At night, satellites streak across the heavens and I wince.

I feel a keening within me. My hearing is more acute, my nose savors the smells, my eyes are sharp, my heart at ease.

I think of a man I once read of in a small book. The man had the kind of name that makes modern people laugh when they hear it, a name that sounds like an invention of, say, Hans Christian Andersen or the brothers Grimm. I will speak of him in a moment. But right now I simply remember his words, now centuries old, and I realize how far I must go. But at least I sense I have begun the journey.

I must learn from the wolf.

I am the interloper.

And this is as it should be.

BEETLE-TRACKED DUNES, WITH THE SIERRA ENTERRADA IN THE BACKGROUND. GRAN DESIERTO

EVENING PRIMROSE, SAND VERBENA, AND STICKLEAF FLOWER ABUNDANTLY AMONG THE DUNES OF GRAN DESIERTO AFTER WINTER RAINS.

FLOWERING LUPINE (*Lupinus sp.*) AND BRITTLEBUSH MIX WITH SENITA CACTUS (*Lophocereus schottii*). SIERRA PINACATE, PINACATE PROTECTED ZONE

GLOBEMALLOW (*Sphaeralcea ambigua*) AND BRITTLEBUSH (*Encelia farinosa*) BLOOM AT THE EDGE OF A LAVA FLOW.
NEAR CARNEGIE PEAK IN THE SIERRA PINACATE, PINACATE PROTECTED ZONE

BRITTLEBUSH BLOOMS AMID SENITA CACTUS WITH RED LAVA IN THE BACKGROUND. SIERRA PINACATE, PINACATE PROTECTED ZONE

A DOWNED OCOTILLO (*Fouquieria splendens*) WITH CHOLLAS AGAINST THE BLACK VOLCANIC ASH. PINACATE PROTECTED ZONE

A FALLEN AND DECAYING SAGUARO CACTUS AGAINST VOLCANIC ASH. PINACATE PROTECTED ZONE

BRITTLEBUSH, OCOTILLO AND A LONE SAGUARO CACTUS. CARNEGIE PEAK, SIERRA PINACATE, PINACATE PROTECTED ZONE

HEARTLEAF EVENING PRIMROSE (*Camissonia cardiophylla*) GROWING ON A LAVA FLOW BENEATH CARNEGIE PEAK, PINACATE PROTECTED ZONE

GLOBEMALLOW GROWING IN THE LAVA FLOWS NEAR CARNEGIE PEAK. SIERRA PINACATE, PINACATE PROTECTED ZONE

NUT SEDGE (*Cyperus* sp.) LINES THE BOTTOM OF DIABLITO CANYON. PARQUE NACIONAL SIERRA SAN PEDRO MARTIR

FROM LEFT TO RIGHT: VARIOUS *Horsfordia* SPECIES, DESERT LAVENDER (*Hyptis emoryi*), AND *Bebbia juncea* APPEAR AT FIRST LIGHT ON A LAVA TANK WALL.
AT TINAJA EMILIA IN THE SIERRA PINACATE, PINACATE PROTECTED ZONE

COYOTE GOURD (*Curcurbita palmata*) FLOWERS AMID STREAMBED GRANITE IN DIABLITO CANYON. PARQUE NACIONAL SIERRA SAN PEDRO MARTIR

PLANTS THAT OCCUR IN BOTH THE SONORAN DESERT AND THE TROPICAL DECIDUOUS FOREST ARE
SONORAN ORGANPIPE CACTUS AND QUEEN'S-WREATH (*Antigonon leptopus*). RIO MAYO DRAINAGE AREA

A SIERRA PINACATE LAVA FLOW PUNCTUATED WITH ISLANDS OF FLOWERING BRITTLEBUSH. PINACATE PROTECTED ZONE

WHITE BRITTLEBUSH EDGES THE VOLCANIC CRATER CERRO COLORADO. PINACATE PROTECTED ZONE

BRITTLEBUSH IN FLOWER WITH SENITA AMID LAVA BLOCKS. CARNEGIE PEAK, SIERRA PINACATE, PINACATE PROTECTED ZONE

NEAR CARNEGIE PEAK, BRITTLEBUSH AND LUPINE BLOOM. SENITA CACTUS IN BACKGROUND. SIERRA PINACATE, PINACATE PROTECTED ZONE

A SENITA SKELETON ON VOLCANIC ASH. SIERRA PINACATE, PINACATE PROTECTED ZONE

GRANITE BOULDERS WITH HUMMINGBIRD BUSH *(Calliandra californica)* AND ELEPHANT TREE *(Pachycormus discolor)*. DESIERTO CENTRAL, NEAR CATAVIÑA

ELEPHANT TREES (*Pachycormus discolor*) LEFT, (*Bursera microphilia*), AND CARDÓN CACTUS (*Pachycereus pringlei*) AT SUNRISE WITH
TRES VIRGENES IN THE BACKGROUND, BAJA SUR

BURSERA ODORATA WITH ORGANPIPE CACTUS (*Cereus thurberi*) ABOVE MANGROVE SHORE. BAJA CALIFORNIA SUR, BAHIA CONCEPCION,
ISLAND OF EL REQUESON IN THE SEA OF CORTEZ

ROCK FIG (*Ficus palmeri*) ROOTED IN LAVA OF THE TRES VIRGENES VOLCANOS. BAJA SUR

TRES VIRGENES, BAJA SUR, INACTIVE VOLCANOES

SAND VERBENA (*Abronia villosa*) BLOOMS NEAR SILVER CHOLLA (*Opuntia echinocarpa*). VIZCAÍNO DESERT, BAJA CALIFORNIA

EVENING PRIMROSE, MORNING FOG'S DEW, AND QUAIL TRACKS MARK THE SAND NEAR THE SEA OF CORTEZ. PUERTO LOBOS

A SUN-WEATHERED AND CONTORTED BARREL CACTUS (*Ferocactus peninsulae*). SIERRA AGUA VERDE, BAJA SUR

WRINKLED, DYING, AND COLORED BY THE SUN ARE LEAVES OF AGAVE (*Agave shawii*). SIERRA SAN BORJA

NIGHTSHADE *(Solanum hindsianum)* FLOWERS AGAINST A MASSIVE CARDÓN CACTUS *(Pachycereus pringlei)*. DESIERTO CENTRAL, NEAR CATAVIÑA

ISLA ANGEL DE LA GUARDA IN THE SEA OF CORTEZ

THE VIZCAÍNO DESERT. SIERRA AGUA VERDE, BAJA SUR

NEAR PUERTO LOBOS ON THE SEA OF CORTEZ

53

THE SUN-BLEACHED SIDE OF A CARDÓN CACTUS. DESIERTO CENTRAL

A SUN-REDDENED CARDÓN CACTUS. SIERRA LA GIGANTA, BAJA SUR

SURF OF THE SEA OF CORTEZ AT BAHIA DE SANTA INES POUNDS ON VOLCANIC ROCK AS A THUNDERSTORM CRASHES IN THE DISTANCE. PUNTA CHIVATO, BAJA SUR

AT CABO SAN LUCAS, THE VERY TIP OF BAJA SUR

NEAR LORETO, SEA OF CORTEZ

SCAMMON'S LAGOON (Laguna Ojo de Liebre), FAVORED AREA FOR THE GRAY WHALE. BAJA SUR

ORGANPIPE CACTUS ROOTED IN VOLCANIC ROCK. SEA OF CORTEZ, BAJA SUR

ISLA ANGEL DE LA GUARDA IN THE SEA OF CORTEZ

A FOREST OF CARDÓN CACTUS AND WHITE-BARKED PALO BLANCO TREES (*Lysiloma candida*) AT SUNRISE. IN THE BACKGROUND IS SIERRA LA GIGANTA. BAJA SUR

ISLA ANGEL DE LA GUARDA GLOWS AT SUNSET IN BAHIA DE LOS ANGELES. BAJA CALIFORNIA

PAINTED DESERT, LIMBERBUSH (*Jatropha cuneata*), AND OCOTILLO (*Fouquieria diguetii*). NEAR SAN EVARISTO, BAJA SUR

BOOJUM *(Fouquiera columnaris)* WITH LICHEN *(Ramalina reticulata)* IN MORNING FOG NEAR EL ROSARIO. DESIERTO CENTRAL, BAJA CALIFORNIA

GRANITE BOULDERS, SENITA CACTUS, AND BOOJUM. DESIERTO CENTRAL, NEAR CATAVIÑA

YUCCA, BOOJUM, AND CARDÓN CACTUS IN THE MORNING LIGHT. SIERRA SAN BORJA

NEAR CATAVIÑA

CATAVIÑA GOLDEN EYE AT THE BASE OF BOOJUM WITH CARDÓN CACTUS. BAJA CALIFORNIA

DESIERTO CENTRAL, NEAR CATAVIÑA

BOOJUM IN THE DESIERTO CENTRAL NEAR CATAVIÑA

JOSHUA TREE NATIONAL MONUMENT

TWO

The body is small, the face hidden in a beard and no one ever makes out his features. When he enters a house, he frightens everyone. He carries a torch and he does as he chooses. "There, see that man?" the visitor seems to say. He seizes him, makes three deep gashes in his body, rips out his entrails, cuts off a portion, and tosses them on the fire to cook. He grabs another man, slashes again, and removes the elbow. Later, merely with his touch, these grotesque wounds are instantly healed. Sometimes he lifts houses up and casts them down, sometimes he appears at the dances in the dress of a woman; at other times garbed like a man. He never eats food. When people ask where he came from, he shows them all a deep crack in the earth and says his home is below.

Of course, all this happened years ago, ten years perhaps, fifteen, who truly knows? Doubters of this tale must face the evidence—the victims of this visitor were brought forth, the gashes from the savage wounds were displayed as proof. The strange man with the small body and the beard and the features no one could ever quite discern, he is remembered simply as Badthing.

The people explain these events to new visitors. And these new visitors are our link because they know how to write, because they hail from a European culture we have largely inherited. The year? Oh, maybe A.D. 1535. The place somewhere on the coastal belt of Texas. It is all very vague because no one telling the story or hearing the story has much need of time anymore. As one of the visitors wrote years later,

ALL THE INDIANS OF THIS REGION ARE IGNORANT OF TIME, EITHER BY THE SUN OR THE MOON; NOR DO THEY RECKON BY THE MONTH OR YEAR. THEY UNDERSTAND THE SEASONS IN TERMS OF THE RIPENING OF THE FRUITS, THE DYING OF FISH, AND THE POSITION OF THE STARS, IN WHICH DATING THEY ARE ADEPT.[4]

The visitors are three Spaniards and one Moor, who is their slave. The leader of the group is a man called Alvar Núñez Cabeza de Vaca. They are the residue of a once larger human swarm. In 1528 five hundred men with horses and arms had landed on the coast of Florida seeking to conquer fat kingdoms, find gold, and become rich beyond men's dreams. The swamps kill them with hunger and fevers. The native people kill them with arrows. The ships that leave them off for their campaign can never discover them again. Some say there is a curse on this adventure, that a Moorish woman back in Spain had predicted it would all come to ruin. The bravos who march off into the bogs and palmetto groves leave ten wives back aboard the ships. The women know. Within days they have taken new husbands. Some, more reluctant to break their vows, choose to be simply concubines. All know the backs of their men are the last they will see of them.

The men themselves are a type and Cabeza de Vaca is in some ways the essence of this type. Cervantes himself etched their character perfectly in his description of America:

THE RECOURSE OF THE RUINED, THE REFUGE AND SHELTER OF THE DESPERATE MEN OF SPAIN, THE SANCTUARY OF THE FRAUDULENT BANKRUPTS, THE PARDON OF MURDERS, THE HAVEN OF LOOSE WOMEN, THE LAST TRICK OF GAMBLERS, THE COMMON CHEAT OF MANY AND THE REMEDY OF FEW.[5]

The strange name Cabeza de Vaca (Head of the Cow) comes from a thirteenth-century ancestor, a miserable shepherd who showed his king a secret mountain pass marked by a steer's skull. The king led an army through the pass, conquered the dreaded Moors, and bequeathed on the peasant a new name. Since then the family has risen, but not so much, and now in the 1530s is part of that class of low gentry who hunger for blood and adventure, cherish honor, and have purses with very little money. The same stamp of human beings who have recently sacked the islands of the Caribbean and laid waste to the universe called Mexico. Cabeza de Vaca's grandfather conquered the Canary Islands in the late fifteenth century. He was a man of some ferocity—once ripping out a courtier's tongue in Spain for a remark that offended him. Cabeza de Vaca was born about 1490 and raised in his grandfather's house surrounded by slaves from the Canaries, a people with a strange language and sad songs, a folk believed to be descendants of that earlier ruin called Carthage. Cabeza de Vaca himself is blooded, having been at the battle of Ravenna in Italy, where 20,000 Spaniards died in one of the periodic disasters that a warrior culture endured.

He and the dark Moor, Esteban, are the two who truly matter to us. In time one will be conquered by America and the other will be killed by the world that he belonged to for a brief time. They are part of a tiny group of men who have survived the death that claimed five hundred. When Florida proved impossible and the ships never returned, the few hundred that still lived made boats from hides, and this pitiful armada was launched on the Gulf of Mexico hoping to drift to Mexico. Men went mad from thirst, drank their urine, did all the things that usually happen. Finally a small remnant, seventy or eighty, were beached without food or clothing on Galveston Island, or so our best guesses have decided. At first the natives helped them, brought them to their fires, found them food, gave them shelter. But it was not enough. The Europeans continued to die and some, to the horror of the natives, ate their comrades' flesh. A plague hit the island, the Indians insisted Cabeza de Vaca and his few companions become healers. And so they did. But in the end their powers were not sufficient for the task and they were made slaves.

Cabeza de Vaca eventually became a trader, a man who went from tribe to tribe with precious things, shells, bits of this and that. For four years he toiled. This was part of the process that makes us pay attention to him. First, a conquistador, then a shipwreck, then a healer, then a slave. Then a creature of commerce. He tells us how this phase felt:

THIS OCCUPATION SUITED ME; I COULD TRAVEL WHERE I WISHED, WAS NOT OBLIGED TO WORK, AND WAS NOT A SLAVE. WHEREVER I WENT, THE INDIANS TREATED ME HONORABLY AND GAVE ME FOOD, BECAUSE THEY LIKED MY COMMODITIES. THEY WERE GLAD TO SEE ME WHEN I CAME AND DELIGHTED TO BE BROUGHT WHAT THEY WANTED. I BECAME WELL KNOWN. . . . THIS SERVED MY MAIN PURPOSE, WHICH ALL THE WHILE WAS TO DETERMINE AN EVENTUAL ROAD OUT.[6]

Then, in 1532, he and a companion fled toward Mexico and in time hooked up with Esteban and his companion, fellow survivors of the once grand expedition. At this moment, they were in part new men. They had not worn clothing for years, nor felt shoes on their feet, nor known warmth in winter. They seldom had enough food and they had become very hard and could endure things they once could not have imagined.

That is why they interest us. They are being broken down, melted like an old statue, and recast into something new. When they finish this process they will have traveled thousands of miles without shoes or the touch of cloth on their skin. They will have learned six new languages and heard many others. They will have eaten weeds, bugs, seeds, blood, guts, rotten meat. They will not have seen a sign of their own kind or heard the absolution of a priest or heard the bell of a church or sat at a table and eaten off a plate. Cabeza de Vaca will be the first European to have ever been an American or be in America. And he may well have been the last. And he will have looked into the country that long, long afterward we will come to call the Sonoran Desert.

It is odd, but the text that tells us of these men—the centuries-old text—seems immediate. There is something about this particular trek by these particular men that seems to free it from the normal constraints of time. The next phase of their journey begins with a dead man. The three Spaniards still retain the training to protect them from much of their new reality. The Indians? Abject savages ignorant of the true God. The tale of Badthing? Surely, a visit by Satan himself. The disaster of the expedition? Simply the result of a stupid commander, a man they now think drowned somewhere in the Gulf. The task before them is simple—to beat their way through savage nations and back to the embrace of Europeans in Mexico. But the dead man . . .

They had already taken up their earlier ways as healers, making the sign of the cross over various ailing Indians, and the Indians had all been healed. The Spaniards wonder much at this fact. True, they believed in miracles, but such work belonged to saints, and they knew they were not saints, or to priests and clearly they were not priests. But they were survivors and so they healed. Then, Indians from a neighboring village came with news of a dying man. When Cabeza de Vaca got there the man was truly dead, the body cool, the pulse gone, the eyes rolled back up into the head. He prayed anyway, and as he had seen native medicine men do, he made sucking sounds over the corpse as if bringing something bad and dangerous from the body. And the man came back from the dead and lived.

Such is the mercy of God he tells us. But we will never truly know what he thought. He wrote of his journey years later when he was safe again among Europeans, among his fellow countrymen, who would doubtless burn him at a stake if he had said he cured men and raised the dead by his own power, by the force he had learned in the land of the heathen. A hundred years after his death Cabeza de Vaca will still be denounced in his own country and in others for the heresy of these cures. And in our century scholars of various stripes will puzzle over them and, depending upon their own faiths, either assign them to the mercy of God or, if unbelievers, write tirades about simpleminded Indians and the various bugaboos they pawn off as true illness. Few, if any, will confront a different possibility: that this one broken, starving conquistador, this slave with marks of beatings on his emaciated body, had fallen into a new country and tasted a new standing and found a new power.[7]

One spring day in 1535 the time finally comes to go into the true unknown. The four men leave the Indians and strike out, lonely shamans on a vast globe of dirt and water. They will walk two thousand miles before they see their own kind or hear their own language. Their route is still debated—across Texas, then down into Mexico, perhaps up again into New Mexico and Arizona, and finally, everyone agrees, deep into the bones and flesh of Sonora and Sinaloa.

The long walk begins, of course, with healing. Soon a handful of natives follows them about, then hundreds, finally thousands. A moving army, but without weapons. Cabeza de Vaca makes peace between warring tribes, teaching the rudiments of his faith that he himself knows. "Through all these nations," he writes later, "the people who were at war quickly made up so they could come meet us with everything they possessed."[8] The Indians make the sign of the cross by holding their arms out and becoming a living crucifix. Food is shared and none will eat of anything until the holy men have blessed the game brought in by the hunters, the seeds and berries gathered by the women. A curious practice arises. As they enter a village, their followers take everything and leave the inhabitants with nothing. Then the sacked natives join the throng, and at the next village they join the taking and recover goods. When Cabeza de Vaca protests this practice he is told that no one is disturbed, that it is not a problem. And so it continues, as this mass of humans plunges on, an instant community of a type we vaguely know—a kind of Stone Age Woodstock. "The Indians," he tells us, "ever stayed with us until they safely delivered us to others. They were all convinced that we came from Heaven."[9]

The holy men now have a name. Since they come from the east, they are called Children of the Sun. All four are healers now. There is so much work to do that even the Islamic Moor must be allowed to participate and any fine theological points are cast aside in this very new world. The Children of the Sun feel no hunger, nor do they feel cold or heat. They are beyond want and can hardly remember their earlier years in this new land when they wept from hunger and fear, when their comrades died from hardships and literally surrendered the will to live.

They are in Sonora now, that modern Mexican state that shares a name with a vast, hot desert. At a place now called Ures, a town that still exists and can be visited, several things happen. The native people offer up six hundred deer hearts to the multitude and these are divided equally. Cabeza de Vaca notices some malachite arrowheads, thinks they must be emeralds, and is told they come from the north. The heartbeat of the conquistador briefly thuds back to life within him and greed briefly shimmers once again in his imagination. Still, his head is changed, for he says of the natives what few conquistadors could ever admit: "They are a substantial people with a capacity for unlimited development."[10]

They are in the Sonoran Desert now, but they speak little of it. They do not tell of the giant cactus, they leave us practically nothing in the way of a description of the land. This is normal for such men at such a time. The world as we now see it, one rich with metaphors for nature and keen for the feel of wild land, that world does not exist in the minds of Europeans in the sixteenth century. It has yet to be born. Europe seemed to hate nature. By the time of the Doomsday Book in England in 1086 less than two percent of the virgin forest remained. Nature seemed to be the enemy to the puny humans confronting it. By the sixteenth century Henry VIII of England would have two or three hundred deer rounded up, penned, and then amuse himself by watching his dogs rip them to shreds.

BEAVERTAIL CACTUS IN BLOOM (*Opuntia basilaris*) AMID GRANITE. JOSHUA TREE NATIONAL MONUMENT

And this attitude led to a verbal emptiness when confronting this new world across the water. Gonzalo Fernández de Oviedo, a contemporary of Cabeza de Vaca, in writing his history of the conquests confessed that he could not describe landscapes: "Of all the things I have seen, this is the one which has left me without hope of being able to describe it in words."[11] Nor could Columbus, as any reading of his journals will reveal.

Cabeza de Vaca makes a slight mention in his own account of the harsh ground to the west, the strange desert of the boojum, the cardón, the pitihaya, the saguaro, and the people we now call Seris. "The timid, surly Indians of the coast," Cabeza de Vaca records, "grow no corn; they eat powdered rushes, straw, and fish which they catch from rafts, having no canoes. The women cover themselves somewhat with grass and straw." And then nothing but silence.

The Children of the Sun move south and a few days later their new world is upended. They come upon an Indian on the banks of the Yaqui River who has a bent nail and a belt buckle. He describes bearded men who came from the sea, visited the river—where they kindly ran lances through two natives—and then disappeared back onto the waves. They are getting near, they are reaching home, they are coming into their country. "Having almost despaired," Cabeza de Vaca admits, "of finding Christians again, we could hardly restrain our excitement."[12]

Within days they are reassured of the truth of the Indian's story. The land they now cross has hardly a single human being—all have fled to the mountains in terror. Not of the Children of the Sun, but of the others. Spaniards based in Culiacan have been raiding north for slaves and they have laid the land waste: "With heavy hearts we looked over the lavishly watered, fertile, and beautiful land, now abandoned and burned and the people thin or hiding in fright. Not having planted, they were reduced to eating roots and bark; and we shared their famine the whole way. . . . We found survivors too alarmed to stay anywhere very long, unable or unwilling to till, preferring death to a repetition of their recent horror."[13]

This time Badthing cannot simply be explained away as a manifestation of Satan. This time his face is seen, and he wears buckles, makes nails, carries a lance. Natives come to the Children of the Sun and they say that they hid behind trees and saw these bearded strangers marching through the woods carrying away Indians in chains. The mob of people with Cabeza de Vaca and his companions are terrified. Then it happens. Some day toward the end of March in the year 1536, they come upon men on horseback. They are somewhere in what we now call Sinaloa.

Four men step forward from an Indian throng. They wear nothing. Their feet are like clubs. They begin to speak in Spanish and Cabeza de Vaca says his first sentence, "Take me to your captain," who turns out to be an unusually weak and vicious conquistador, Diego de Alcazar. The Children of the Sun now stare into the face that they once wore.

The slavers look upon their multitudes and think one thought: to make them slaves. Cabeza de Vaca is appalled. This cannot be. The Spaniards argue with the Indians and say that they are true Christians and that the Children of the Sun are not the real power in this place.

ALCAZAR BADE HIS INTERPRETER TELL THE INDIANS THAT WE WERE MEMBERS OF HIS RACE WHO HAD BEEN LONG LOST; THAT HIS GROUP WERE THE LORDS OF THE LAND WHO MUST BE OBEYED AND SERVED, WHILE WE WERE INCONSEQUENTIAL. THE INDIANS PAID NO ATTENTION TO THIS. CONFERRING AMONG THEMSELVES, THEY REPLIED THAT THE CHRISTIANS LIED: WE HAD COME FROM THE SUNRISE, THEY FROM THE SUNSET; WE HEALED THE SICK, THEY KILLED THE SOUND; WE CAME NAKED AND BAREFOOT, THEY CLOTHED, HORSED, AND LANCED; WE COVETED NOTHING BUT GAVE WHATEVER WE WERE GIVEN, WHILE THEY ROBBED WHOMEVER THEY FOUND AND BESTOWED NOTHING ON ANYONE.[14]

For one brief instant two worlds gaze into each other and then the accommodation begins. Cabeza de Vaca and his companions are tricked by the false promises of the Spaniards and taken south to Culiacan. Their followers are left behind and once the four Children of the Sun are out of sight, the conquistadors briefly make them all slaves. When Cabeza de Vaca and his companions discover this, they protest to the local authority, a conquistador named Melchior Díaz who ranks above Alcazar. The Indians, these converts to a faith embodied by four naked Europeans, are swiftly freed. The long journey of the Children of the Sun is over. For a while, Cabeza de Vaca cannot bear the touch of cloth to his skin, nor can he sleep in a bed. This passes. By the time he gets to Mexico City, he is wardrobed by grandees, feted by the Viceroy. He apparently lets slip stories that he heard from his followers of large towns to the north of his path, of seven cities to be exact. These words cause notice.

His two Spanish companions settle down and slip from the notice of history. Esteban, the Moor, lingers in the New World, still a slave. His survival of the trek across North America does not win him his freedom, a fact that across the centuries still seems an unpardonable wrong. Cabeza de Vaca himself returns to his wife and monarch in Spain. Several years later he is sent out as the new governor of Paraguay. He begins the thousand-mile walk into the country at the head of two hundred fifty armed men by pausing and removing his shoes. He makes the journey barefoot and with no problem from the natives. Later, he is seized, imprisoned, and sent home in chains. The charges are complicated, but they all revolve around his kindness to the Indians, his abhorrence of slavery. He is a victim of what he has seen and learned. He dies sometime in the 1560s disgraced, stripped of power, broken financially, and forgotten.

Only a brief book he published in 1542 (and revised later to include his time in Paraguay) remains. It is the story of a man who enters a new world and is slowly cleansed of the pollution he brings with him. Of a man who wanders for years in the country, who heals, who stops conflict, who becomes a child of the sun. Of a man who glimpses the Sonoran Desert but says little of this hot ground since he lacks the vocabulary to describe it, as does the culture of the Europe that has created him.

No one really knows what to make of his little book. How can we? Few have been to the place he visited or are willing to lay down the miles to get there. He lingers now as an embarrassing ghost in our historical attic, the man conquered by America, the odd fellow who did not know the power of our ways. Now we dote on old mission buildings, glass cases where we store ancient armor, tales of conquistadors, hymns about frontiers and progress and the days of settlement. We restore old colonial homes and imagine that we, too, are grandees of Spain.

A quarter century ago, William Woodruff tried to capture this part of ourselves:

NO CIVILIZATION PRIOR TO THE EUROPEAN HAD OCCASION TO BELIEVE IN THE SYSTEMATIC MATERIAL PROGRESS OF THE WHOLE HUMAN RACE; NO CIVILIZATION PLACED SUCH STRESS UPON THE QUANTITY RATHER THAN THE QUALITY OF LIFE; NO CIVILIZATION DROVE ITSELF SO RELENTLESSLY TO AN EVER RECEDING GOAL; NO CIVILIZATION WAS SO PASSION-CHARGED TO REPLACE WHAT IS WITH WHAT COULD BE; NO CIVILIZATION HAD STRIVEN AS THE WEST HAS DONE TO DIRECT THE WORLD ACCORDING TO ITS WILL; NO CIVILIZATION HAS KNOWN SO FEW MOMENTS OF PEACE AND TRANQUILITY.[15]

When we say we wish to know the Sonoran Desert, we must not forget these facts. When we say we wish to see the Sonoran Desert, we must not forget these masks that blind our eyes. When we say we wish to save the Sonoran Desert, we must not forget the deep wellsprings of our power that poison us with the myth that we can mold and determine other worlds, nations, bloods.

We should recall Cabeza de Vaca, even though he left us but a few scraps of fact about this slab of hot, dry ground. We do not need his facts. We do not care where he camped, how many leagues he made this day or that. Whether Badthing was a force of Satan.

We begin to walk, the ground burns through the soles of our shoes, the brush claws at our flesh, ants are busy everywhere on the ground and white light seems to sear our eyes. We worry at the canteen in our pack, wonder at our path as the ground closes in behind us. A saguaro towers over us, the skin a waxed green. It will not tell us of its years. It will not tell us its thoughts. Of course, we know it cannot think. It is not like us.

We walk on and go farther. Perhaps we should take off these shoes. And then in a few miles, the shirt. The trousers. Feel the sun on our skin, taste thirst, eye the lizard with our mouths dry and our bellies empty.

Burn the books. No? Well, that can wait. The paper may prove useful.

Walk on.

THREE

There are many ways to come into this country and few ways to stay. For many, like the early Spaniards, there never seemed to be enough here, not enough silver, not enough slaves, and so they would march on always looking, looking, looking. For others, there is never enough anywhere else. I remember once giving a talk on the Tohono O'odham reservation in southern Arizona, a place about the size of Connecticut that is seldom visited by outsiders and that O'odham seem hardly able to leave.

When I got to the meeting the room was cold linoleum floors, cold light from fluorescent wands, cold tabletops, cold chairs. And brown faces. A Tohono O'odham was talking slowly and softly and one waited for each word, a small cloud of sound that floated across the cold room. He wore his hair long in the manner of dead ancestors. He was about forty and, my God, the words were so soft I could hardly hear them. "We have these legends, these myths," he whispered, "stories told by the elders. We know how it will end. This all must go, this is the Third World. It will go. Flood, fire, there will be a way. It will go."

As he spoke a video camera hummed on, the lens pivoting from my face to his and back again. Everything was being recorded. It was a very cold room.

"Some," he said, the words fluttering from his lips and drifting to the floor, "some will survive. They will live to see the Fourth World."

I nodded. But what about this world? What about the dead Indian they are digging that grave for a hundred yards down the road? The one killed in a fight. What about the drunks, what about the boy, you remember the boy, who left the family table in this village and walked off into the night and was found in the morning hanging from a mesquite tree, the cord of a toaster wound around his neck?

"You plan," the voice whispered, "for ten years, or twenty years, or thirty years. We must think seven generations ahead. That is what the elders say."

He lit a Camel cigarette as he spoke.

It is easy to dismiss such talk as just that, talk. But what strikes me is that I don't know any person or organization that plans for seven generations. The plants out there in the desert, perhaps. After all, a saguaro lives about 200 years and casts down maybe a hundred million to two hundred million seeds during its lifetime in an effort to replicate itself. The animals, of them I cannot say, they do not speak to us—although I am struck by our failure to exterminate the coyote. But what I heard that day was offered as one way of staying—century after century. Think seven generations ahead, watch one world collapse into the next. Light a cigarette.

Go crazy. Yes, crazy. One of the interesting points about desert people in the past, and in some instances in the present, is that the world could (and can) make them sick; the living, breathing world could strike them down. All kinds of native creatures had power and, if offended, could cripple a human with fever, weakness, or other maladies. We have libraries full of such accounts. When we came here this began to change. Consider horses in their eyes. Like all animals, horses cause disease, in this case insanity—the white man's animal brings the white man's plague. The cure is only possible through songs and the songs can only be had from yet another white innovation, the devil. The Tohono O'odham took their music where they could.

An anthropologist, Ruth Underhill, was out with the desert people in the 1930s. She listened, sometimes asked, but mainly listened to the monotone voices letting slip little fragments of their dreamtime. There was this singer who knew horse songs. Underhill listened, the singer explained:

I ONCE FELL FROM A HORSE AND WAS UNCONSCIOUS FOR TWENTY-FOUR HOURS. DURING THAT TIME, DEVILS CAME TO ME. THEY WERE DRESSED LIKE MEXICANS AND HAD YELLOWISH FACES AND MUSTACHES. THEY WERE RIDING HORSES AND HAD A SPARE HORSE FOR ME. WE RODE INSIDE OF THE MOUNTAIN RANGES AND SAW THE GOLD AND SILVER PILED UP THERE. THEY SANG AND I LEARNED THEIR SONGS. WHEN I CAME TO, I WAS SINGING THEM.

NOW EVERY NIGHT AS I FALL ASLEEP I HEAR THEM SINGING, FAR OFF. IT IS A NEW SONG, AND I LEARN IT AS THEY APPROACH. WHEN THEY ARRIVE I KNOW IT, AND WE GO OFF SINGING TOGETHER. SOMETIMES I DON'T REMEMBER THE SONG IN THE MORNING; OFTEN I DO.

We have lost such forms of sickness. We can kill, mold, develop, bulldoze—and what we fear is industrial injury and the hard faces of bankers foreclosing on us. We do not fear anything out there in any deep sense. The scorpion may sting, but we have these drugs, we tell ourselves.

Down on the peninsula of Baja, another way of staying was recorded. It is a way few human cultures would pick, and in the desert all may well experience the fate of this culture—extinction. On this thin peninsula, Spaniards met a group that clearly appalled them. After having sacked most of a hemisphere, having met more tribes than they could remember, destroyed cultures so thoroughly that sometimes not a single scrap of their language has survived,[16] still the Spaniards were not ready for this small group of people.

These people build no homes and will not leave the ground where they are born. They wear nothing, plant nothing, and tell the Spaniards little of what is in their minds. They resist the missionaries. They tie meat to a string, chew and swallow it, then pull it up and dine again. They save their excrement during the season of the cactus fruit, dry it, grind up any undigested seeds into a rich paste, make a drink, and swallow. For property, they carry a tray, a bowl, a small stick for fire making, an awl fashioned from a sharp bone, a net. They seem uninterested in marriage vows. They kill and eat everything but the badger and the lion. Though they are a day's walk from the sea, some say they have never been to it. They are called Pericue and centuries later scholars will think they are a remnant of the earliest people, a link now broken in the chain of life.

We will never find out who they were. And when they are gone they will leave nothing behind but a few hard words scribbled by Spaniards who had to deal with them.

There is one haunting image of the vanished group. In the 1880s two Frenchmen wander Baja and in a small village come upon a woman. She has a pyramidal skull and does not look like the other villagers. She tells the visitors very little. Supposedly, the Pericue have been gone for more than a century, wiped out by diseases of white men and the weapons of everyone. No one will care about their demise for several more decades, when—suddenly—modern anthropology will sense the lost tribe is a link to very early human beings.

Such matters do not concern the woman. She simply is. They ask for permission to take her photo. She refuses. And then they leave, convinced they have found the last member of a culture, and that is the end of her. She is perhaps the last Pericue.

And so the Pericue managed to stay on this hard ground, but only by being unbending, by dying out, by mingling their bones with the dust, by never succumbing to our blandishments. I am happy the photograph was never taken, that the skull was not meticulously measured for anthropology, that the woman, whatever her bloodlines, went to an unknown grave to embrace whatever gods awaited her. That she stayed, forever, in this desert we both love.

But what of us, invaders with our baggage of gods, solid houses, elaborate communications systems, sense of power and mastery—is there any way we may stay, or are we merely a brief episode in a place where a few sane Homo sapiens say they think seven generations ahead, and plants and animals keep their own counsel?

If we look down at the ground we may find some help. One mention of some fellow desert residents comes from Guatemala in a book called Popul Vuh, *stories of the Maya first recorded by Dominican friars in the sixteenth century. We like to call these records myths. Hunahpu and Xbalanqué have been taken prisoner by Hun-Camé and Vukub-Camé. They will be killed unless they can fill four vases with flowers. Of course, they are kept under guard and close confinement—all true contests must have an edge.[17] So the two men call for their allies, the fungus-growing ants of the tropics, which we call leaf-cutter ants. And the ants toil all night, sacking the garden that belongs to the very two princes who hold their friends captive. The garden is under heavy guard, but this does not matter. The ants work silently and with great cooperation through the dark hours. With first light, the vases are filled and the captors humiliated when presented with the blossoms of their own garden. Thus, the fungus-growing ants made their first known appearance in human literature.*

There are other references to them in the early records of the Spaniards, cries of outrage over the damage the ants could do, odd notes such as that some of the native Americans used the ants in surgery by letting the huge soldier ants bite the flesh, then breaking off their giant heads and thus suturing the wound. For centuries no one knew much about the ants except that they could strip a garden overnight.

In 1874 Thomas Belt published an odd volume entitled The Naturalist in Nicaragua, *a book that details his many bizarre days digging up ant colonies. He speculated that the ants did not really eat leaves but simply used them to grow fungus. In 1893 the Berlin Academy of Sciences gave Alfred Moeller five thousand marks and told him to go to Brazil and figure out just what these ants were up to. He confirmed their fungus-eating habits.*

Though based in the tropics, the ants have adapted to the desert and have penetrated into the United States. They live in huge chambers underground, each chamber connected by tunnels. In southern Sonora these caverns can grow so large that sometimes the corners of buildings sink down when the caverns give way.

Outside Tucson I have watched a colony at work in the laboratory of the Sonoran Arthropod Studies Inc.,[18] one of those better notions in this century, the only organization of its kind in the United States dedicated to nothing but the wonders of bugs. Here the colony lives in plain view in a terrarium with clear plastic pipes leading out of the building and into the desert where they forage.

The effort is divided among various types of workers, the inevitable fierce-looking soldier to guard the enterprise, and the fertile queen continually laying eggs. A stream of ants constantly enters the colony, each incoming member brandishing a portion of a cut leaf. These are worked over and over until they become soft, mushy pellets—a task that can take a single ant fifteen minutes. Then they are carried down to the gardens, underground chambers where the pellets are arranged. A worker has been observed poking a pellet into the tapestry of the garden and then gently patting it into place with its legs. A pellet placed in the morning hours is rife with fungus by afternoon. That is part of the problem, the garden must be constantly weeded by small workers who mow down any fungus resulting from undesired spores. The fungus culture is kept pure, more pure than, say, a human-planted field of wheat. All this work goes forth by means of scent communications; more than twenty separate signals have been observed to date.

Moeller, mad scientist that he was for the Berlin Academy of Sciences, wanted to know what would happen if he reduced the number of toilers in the fungus garden. Normally, the ants are kept hopping just by the task of weeding the crop and snapping off rapid growth in the fungus. But if their numbers are radically reduced, he noted, "the ants are unable to move about in the dense growth of sprouting filaments and have to beat a retreat before the rapidly rising hyphal forest. This, however, as soon as it has acquired a little headway, proliferates mightily, and it is an amazing sight to behold the poor insects, tirelessly active till the last moment, fleeing before their own food plant. If some of the larvae and pupae are still present, they are rescued. The last resort is the vertical wall of the glass up which the insects creep and where they huddle together, while over the wide plain of the garden the fungus proceeds to the [next] stage."

God help us if the ants ever decide to study Homo sapiens with the same objective interest in fostering the ruin of our cities in the hope of adding some quaint little monograph to their own library of science.[19]

When the first rains come in the summer at that hour before dawn, there is an explosion of life flinging up out of the ground—the nuptial flight of the virgin queens, who in a brief hour mate and set out to found new colonies. As for the desert itself, these ant colonies function as compost heaps where the organic matter of the surface is constantly being recycled to the roots of the floral world. Perhaps it is merely a trivial detail that our culture's interest in insects pretty much stops with exterminating companies and that the Tohono O'odham believe that ants literally created the world by fabricating a ball of resin from a creosote branch.

Of the very few ways of staying in this desert, of really belonging, this is the third way, the hardest, the one we always try to avoid—to fit into the land, to take no more than we give back, to tend our gardens but not try to make the entire landscape like our garden. Of course, we are not ants, any more than we are coyotes or cacti or mesquites. Nor can we ever be. This is our favorite tactic for dismissing such examples from the natural world, or from other cultures for that matter. It is a feeble thrust. We are animals, perhaps animals gone berserk, but still animals, and the sooner we get back in touch with this fact, the better off we will be. We do not have a free pass from God or various graduate schools to do whatever we wish with this planet. These things we should consider if we wish to stick in this place.

Ah, but we have made a career out of refusing to adapt. We say it is contrary to our custom. One glance at our towns and cities in the region makes this clear. They are all oases, space colonies implanted on what we seem to take to be the forbidding surface of Mars. Even when we try to fit in—with our gestures toward natural history, our science, our ecology, our environmental politics—we still seem to miss the point. The desert does not need us and in time, given our habits, will crush us and reject us. We do not plan for seven generations, we do not seem to give. That willingness apparently ended with Cabeza de Vaca.

This is rather a striking fact. Especially when one considers that much of the flora and fauna of this place did not originate here, but came to this place. (In a sense the place came to them as it has gradually and episodically dried out over the last ten thousand years.) Yet these plants and animals in general, like the tropical fungus-growing ants in particular, have managed to find a world here, have managed to fit into the flow of things.

Perhaps part of the problem is that we no longer dream. A shaman of the Yuma tribe long ago said a thing most of us would certainly find absurd: "Before I was born I would sometimes steal out of my mother's womb while she was sleeping, but it was dark and I did not go far. Every good doctor begins to understand before he is born." There are other strange utterances gathered by our people when they met other people on this ground. They are gathered in old books that are seldom read and that gather dust on the library shelves.

One such statement comes from the Roaring Twenties when a scholar jotted down the words of I'itoi, the Elder Brother or Moses figure of the Piman people, a language grouping that includes the Tohono O'odham and the Pimas among others. The words are old, according to the shaman.

OTHER PEOPLE WILL DO THE THING THAT WE MUST NOT DO,

NAMELY KILL THE EARTH.

AND YOU WILL NOT BE THE ONES TO KILL THE STAYING EARTH.

I WILL LEAVE IT TO THEM.

AND THEY WILL DO IT.

AND THESE WILL KILL THE STAYING EARTH.

AND EVEN IF YOU DON'T KNOW ANYTHING

AND YOU JUST BE FEELING FINE

AND YOU WILL SEE IT WHEN IT HAPPENS.

Just to the west of the Pimas, scholars visited the Maricopas and they said something different.

THE WHITE PEOPLE WERE THE VERY LAST TO SPEAK. IT WAS SAID THAT LIKE A YOUNGER CHILD THEY WERE CRY BABIES. SO THE CREATOR DID EVERYTHING TO SOOTHE THEM. HENCE, THEY ARE RICHER THAN ANY OF THE INDIANS.

My stereo plays in the background. I stare down at the words and decide to have dinner and a good glass of wine. Outside the window, the summer rains build but still there is no relief. But soon it will come, and the ants will dance in courtship in that hour before dawn.

SUNFLOWERS *(Helianthus niveus — subspecies tephrodes)* ANCHORED BY ELONGATED ROOTS IN THE ALGODONES DUNES NATURAL AREA, BUREAU OF LAND MANAGEMENT

GRANITE BOULDERS WITH TURPENTINE BUSH (*Ericameria cuneata*) AT SUNRISE. JOSHUA TREE NATIONAL MONUMENT

BACKED BY THE CHOCOLATE MOUNTAINS ARE THE ALGODONES DUNES IN A BUREAU OF LAND MANAGEMENT NATURAL AREA OF CALIFORNIA

BLUE-GRAY BADLANDS, DESERT HOLLY (*Atriplex hymenelytra*) AND IRONWOOD TREES (*Olneya tesota*). PICACHO STATE RECREATION AREA

DESERT HOLLY. PICACHO STATE RECREATION AREA, CALIFORNIA

UNA PALMA, A LONE CALIFORNIA FAN PALM (*Washingtonia filifera*), IN BORREGO BADLANDS. ANZA-BORREGO DESERT STATE PARK

CALIFORNIA FAN PALMS AT MOUNTAIN PALM SPRINGS IN ANZA-BORREGO DESERT STATE PARK

TAYLOR LAKE AT DAWN WITH COLORADO RIVER AND IMPERIAL NATIONAL WILDLIFE REFUGE IN BACKGROUND. PICACHO STATE RECREATIONAL AREA, CALIFORNIA

SAND BAR PATTERNS AT MID-STREAM OF THE COLORADO RIVER WITH ROCKY CRAIGS OF ARIZONA'S IMPERIAL NATIONAL WILDLIFE REFUGE

SANDSTONE CONCRETIONS IN THE PUMPKIN PATCH, ADJACENT TO ANZA-BORREGO DESERT STATE PARK

ALGODONES DUNES NATURAL AREA, BUREAU OF LAND MANAGEMENT

PRICKLYPEAR CACTUS AND BLOOMING PHACELIA (*Phacelia crenulata*). SAGUARO NATIONAL MONUMENT, TUSCON MOUNTAINS UNIT

FOUR

*H*e called himself Tejo and in 1530 he told the Spaniards that as a boy he had accompanied his Indian father to a place forty days to the north where the natives had abundant silver and lived in cities. [20] Seven cities he said. So Nuño de Guzmán, a great rival of Cortez, set forth with Tejo, four hundred Spaniards, and twenty thousand Indian allies. When they arrived at the place where the city of Culiacan would be eventually planted, they found the going rough because of the many mountains and the expedition ended in failure. Except that Culiacan became the most northern outpost in the new kingdom of Mexico and Guzmán became its great lord. Tejo died and so the tale seemed ended. Guzmán turned to slaving, and thus he was occupied when Cabeza de Vaca and the other Children of the Sun entered his realm in 1536. But word of his actions got back to Mexico City, Cabeza de Vaca himself took notes, and he was recalled, jailed, and cast into disgrace.

A new man was sent forth to end this slaving and establish a new relationship with the Indians, Francisco Vázquez de Coronado, a man but twenty-eight years old in April 1539 and married to a rich widow. He was appointed governor of the province. He traveled to Culiacan that same spring in company with Fray Marcos de Niza and the Moor Esteban. The priest and Esteban were marching to the far north, charged by the Viceroy with checking out the stories of some great towns that Cabeza de Vaca had supposedly mentioned in asides. The Spaniards of the colony thought that these stories seemed to verify the earlier reports of Tejo. Esteban was killed at the pueblo of Zuni in New Mexico, where it is said his arrogance, coupled with his appetite for women, lost him the respect of the inhabitants. His behavior is very hard to judge across the centuries, since he was a slave. His contemporaries and the scholars that have followed in their wake tend to refer to him as the black. He is portrayed as childlike at times; he liked to dance; he liked women. Indians liked him. Whatever his character, he managed to survive one of the greatest human journeys of which we have a record and finally perished at Zuni. With his death, Fray Marcos, who never entered the Zuni pueblo, but at best saw it from afar—if at all—sped south with the rest of his companions, telling of the fabled Seven Cities of gold. He reentered Culiacan that fall with his claims of vast riches. Coronado dispatched Melchior Díaz (the subordinate of Guzmán who had aided Cabeza de Vaca and his Indian companions) and others to scout out the area. By January 6, 1540, Coronado had been commissioned by the Viceroy to lead a full expedition north to find what all hoped would be the next Mexico.

There were 1,000 horses, 600 pack animals, at least 1,300 Indian allies, and about 300 Spaniards. According to the Viceroy, these were not settled men, but basically the fortune hunters and riffraff the New World attracted. They were the kind of men Viceroys tend to use as cannon fodder. The expedition also had a sea arm, a small fleet that was to support and supply the army along the coast—the Spaniards were innocent of the distance from the Sante Fe and Albuquerque area to the Gulf of California.

The entire enterprise proceeded on a consistently even tone. The fleet couldn't find the army and left a message buried under a tree near present-day Yuma, Arizona. Melchior Díaz leading his column back from Yuma was annoyed by a dog pestering the groups' sheep, threw his lance, lost control of his horse, and somehow impaled himself on his own weapon. He died after much suffering and was buried on the trail. The men Coronado left behind to maintain a defensive fallback position at Ures in northern Sonora (the point where Cabeza de Vaca was greeted with love and six hundred deer hearts) were led by Diego de Alcazar, the very Spaniard who had tried to make Cabeza de Vaca's six hundred followers into slaves. In time the natives rose up, struck Alcazar, with a poison arrow from which he slowly died as his skin rotted off his bones, and left the outpost in ashes.

Coronado himself bumbled around the pueblos of the Rio Grande valley for a while annoying the Indians, snuffing a few revolts, and complaining, along with his troops, about the cold weather. Finally, he and his men followed an Indian named Turk out onto the Great Plains, where they were promised a city of gold. When in Kansas (a spot Coronado found as disappointing as Dorothy would) they saw buffalo and not much else. The Turk confessed he was lying. They strangled him.

The army returned to Mexico having seen much and understood little. There were a spate of hearings to determine if Coronado had done the right thing, a lot of complaints were filed, many documents penned, and then a huge silence about this vast region to the north that had failed to produce instant riches. The second great visit to the desert made a very small impression on the Spaniards. They saw it as an uninhabited wasteland, lacking slaves, gold, emeralds, or silver. We now celebrate their passage with monuments and statues. And no one has raised a hand to this day to remember the people who gave six hundred deer hearts to the Children of the Sun.

We would like to believe that the singular focus and greed of our ancestors is a thing of the past which we have grown beyond. This is our necessary myth. We always place the crime in some buried chunk of the bygone years, so that we can become innocents and, thus, in our own eyes we are simply victims of earlier evil deeds. And truly there are these hard pasts that we can relish if that is our appetite—various mutilations of both the land and the people.

But what we share with these conquistadors is our inability to live in the desert. Just as their entradas and settlements were based on odd concentrations of materials—minerals, slaves—so are our settlements. Our cities live on the edges of the desert (Hermosillo, Tucson, Phoenix) close by rivers that protect us from its fangs, and the blood of these communities is often pumped from deep wells where ancient waters are looted and destroyed in a matter of mere decades. The heart of the desert—the vast reaches of Baja, the burning core of southwestern Arizona, the western and northwestern reaches of Sonora—is no more appealing to our city-planting urges than it was to the conquerors four centuries ago.

And still the gambler's impulse prevails with us. Just as the New World became for the riffraff of Spain a place where they could play their last card, so the Sonoran Desert today seems to invite the most harebrained scams put forth by businessmen fleeing the older settlements of other regions.

MORNING CLOUDS AT HORSESHOE BEND OF THE SALT RIVER. SALT RIVER CANYON WILDERNESS, TONTO NATIONAL FOREST

In the mid-nineteenth century George Kippen crossed this ground and left a diary that is remarkably similar in tone to what we might make today of such a journey. It is a record of ruin and schemes. On the third day of July in the year 1855, Kippen was moving slowly eastward from San Diego. He was on his way to mines of the Sonoran Desert, to a place now called Ajo, Arizona. Three days later, as the sun rose, he passed "the body of a Mexican a short distance from the wells who had died from thirst & exhaustion."[21] The next day, "exceedingly hot," he passed eight corpses on the road. The day following he passed a dead man and two dead women. And the day following that he made special note of a corpse— "murdered." By the twelfth of July he had reached the Colorado River near Yuma. Two days later he observed that it was 120 degrees in the shade.

Of the countryside he gives no description. Of the quality of the light, size of the cactus, the birds on the wing, not a mention. In the three hundred and sixty years since Columbus made his landfall, our eyes have not yet improved one whit. Kippen's diary is a rosary which he seems to say each night, and the beads of his prayers are dead men and dead women. A colleague in the mining venture came in out of the desert all but dead from thirst. The man reported another member of the enterprise was undoubtedly dead somewhere back on the trail. This route is now called El Camino del Diablo, the highway of the devil. Today its meanderings are largely encased in federal wildlife refuges and federal parks because the land is so extraordinary.

Kippen held back, leery of moving into the desert. The people who had died from thirst, these gave him pause. As did the heat. And, besides, he confessed he hesitated, "believing my companion mr. Hollings not to be of sound mind." On August 1 he ventured forth. By the third day he paused along the Gila river to give the animals one last good drink— "there being no water for 112 miles and hot as the very devil." Two days later he passed a man who had just died of thirst. By August he made it to water. He was safe. By the seventeenth he noticed his first nondomestic animal— "kill a deer & dry the meat." He repeated the journey several times and the tone remains constant. There is one mention of mesquite beans being good feed for his pack animals. Another time an antelope is shot. A scorpion bites him. There are more bodies along the trail, some killings ("the most horribly cut men that I ever saw!!"). Now and then some Indians drop by to trade and then, apparently without any worry, disappear back into the desert. It is three hundred and ten years since Coronado made his plunge into the region and yet the things noticed and recorded remain remarkably the same. The world we bring to this place cannot face this place.

The Kippens, they come and go. The schemes, they come and go also. The Central Arizona Project, a $5 billion ditch that will cure what ails the desert, Hoover Dam, Glen Canyon Dam, and the like are giant tombstones marking the death of the Colorado River. All this so that we can cure what ails the desert. We make plans for huge toxic waste dumps, things we tell ourselves that cannot possibly harm the desert. After all, there is nothing out there. We are full of schemes for the place we have never been, and barely looked at.

Perhaps this is our stab at the last trick of gamblers. We are truly Coronado's children. Only now we know we should be something else.

FIVE

The rains come when they will, and things live or die because of this fact. No matter. The winds have little effect, they brush against the exterior, but nothing can topple the tower down on the burning earth. When the sun rides low in the sky soft rains fall, and then as the ball of fire rises the moisture ceases and there is nothing but hot wind. When the sun is at its peak in the sky, the rains come again for a while, at least sometimes, and then as it slowly sinks down from the peak and cuts lower and lower arcs, the clouds go away.

Time passes slowly. There is a counting, but it is a different counting. There are names, but many different names—el cirio, Fouquieria columnaris, boojum.22 Imagine a plant that can be seventy-five feet high, maybe a foot and a half or two feet at the base, a form like parsnip jabbing up in the sky, tiny branches, tiny leaves. That is the image. The place is the central desert of Baja California, and one tiny mountain range on the coast of Sonora. The rains by our instruments are maybe three inches a year, or four or five or six inches. Or none at all. The temperatures may reach 120 degrees in summer. This thing called a cirio or a boojum can store some water in its slender column of flesh. It is impervious to wind because it offers little resistance. It is into slow growth, very slow growth. Perhaps eight hundred years pass before it tires of this growing and this living and returns to earth and rots.

No human being has ever found a real use for it, not in thousands of years. The boojum, it is very patient, it seems. We think it has stood on this same ground with very little change in its shape or structure for a hundred million years. Some think two hundred million years. An average of its growth rate renders pitiful little numbers like, say, an eighth of an inch a year. Of course, the cells can make their moves when the rains do come, and the top may shoot up six inches in a favorable season. Then the waiting returns. We refuse to say "the thinking" because we refuse to share the idea of consciousness with the things we call plants. That is why we call them things. In the matter of reproduction, shoots spew out from the top of this parsnip-shaped thing, and flowers appear, and windblown seeds waft across the sky. Maybe every ten or twenty or thirty years, the rains fall just right, the seeds germinate, and the seedlings survive. They are more flexible than we can understand. They thrive in a desert where it never freezes, and yet we know from our experiments they can survive temperatures well below freezing. They survive in a desert where it hardly rains, yet we know that in odd patches where coastal fogs bring moisture they thrive—with balls of lichen hanging off them. There is time, so much time, that it all works out.

For our kind, Homo sapiens, this place and this sense of time can be intolerable. The first Europeans who came here were broken on the wheel of Baja's days and nights. They did not know this would happen. In fact they fought for the chance to come here. Hernan Cortez squandered a fortune trying to settle Baja. He had heard that rich Amazons roamed this ground and he came for them and their wealth. Priests came also, founding missions, rounding up Indians, and then failing. Administrators also floundered in the white light and flaming days. Consider such a man.

Don Gaspar Portola received a reward: he was made the first governor of California, the place we now call Baja. He arrived in Loreto and found a miserable mud fort that baked during the day and was under siege by mosquitoes during the night. He was bored. There was nothing to hunt. There was nowhere to promenade, no games, fetes, balls. There was no one to talk to. He was the boss, and yet all he settled were a few drunken quarrels between local miners. Then, he returned to his slumbers. The days melted into one another, the sea sighed before the town, time barely moved. He was paid 6,000 Rhenish guilders a year and there was nothing to spend it on. His chaplain, Don Fernandez, wanted to flee the place as soon as he arrived. Now he sits silently in his hut, stares at the blue sky and green sea. He strums his guitar.

We wish to laugh at such tales, to mock these earlier men who did not, we think, appreciate the beauty of the place we now call the Sonoran Desert. But then, they were in it, and tasted its flesh. We are merely visitors protected by our machines. We say we wish to strike roots here, to belong. Yes, yes. But think of that odd plant over there, the one with the weird shape waggling into the blue sky. A hundred million years in one place. Striking roots.

The desert is everywhere these days, it has escaped the brown soil and cloudless sky and flown off into the minds of others. I notice this when I travel. I go on business to Washington, D.C., and the desert is waiting for me, packaged and for sale. We have invented a way to be in the desert, to possess the desert, and by looking at it we can finally face what this desert is that we say we possess. In our tongue, the word we relish is nature. The Union Station in Washington, D.C., has recently been restored, the building scrubbed clean, the lobby filled with rare shops. I enter. There are skulls on the wall, the coyote goes for $30, the small cranium looks lacquered, the teeth still sharp. The black bear rug is another matter, $1,100, but think of the thoughts that will flash across your mind as you stretch across it before a blazing wood fire. I feel the thick fur, a voice announces the arrivals and departures of trains.

I ride to Baltimore, the car swaying along the tracks. The office overlooks the harbor from eleven floors up, the wall is glass from floor to ceiling. The man speaking is a lobbyist, about thirty, his accent the nasal bark of Chicago's south side where he made his early bones. He smokes, loosens his tie and we go over the issue. We are at odds here. He has been hired by a university in the desert to help it get support from Congress for a project. I am here as a reporter and I am here to stop both the man and the university he represents. There is this mountain rising up from the desert floor and on its top are many black bears with warm breath still pouring from their mouths, and rare squirrels living in the treetops, moles tunneling under the forest floor, possibly endangered plants, certainly scattered shrines left by earlier Americans, all the usual occupants of what we call unoccupied ground. The mountain is buried under snow now and no one can go there easily until spring. But, of course, this grip of nature will change. It is a new time. His client wants this mountain, must have it, in fact has just taken it from the grasping hands of various federal agencies. Telescopes will impale the peaks, science will be served, the business will go on. Who does not wish to look at the stars? I listen to his words but images get in my way. One is of the mountain if the project is built, a mountain that will be maimed forever and I know it and in my heart I feel that he knows it. This kind of destruction is at the core of modern life and the only thing that really varies is how well a person accepts such havoc. The other images in my mind as he speaks are of an earlier taking and of an earlier destruction. There is this old photo on my wall at home, the grainy image taken about 1902, of two fresh-faced young women, their white blouses full cut, the smiles radiant, their hands in big gloves for riding. They are in a doorway framed by crumbling adobes and they are the conquerors of the desert. Their hips look hungry. One woman is named Mrs. George F. Kitt; her husband's name will become with time Kitt Peak, and Kitt Peak will become with time another warehouse of telescopes, a planetary center of our lust for seeking other planets. Their hips, those young eager hips of the women, brush against my face as I listen to the lobbyist explain his strategy in the office so far from mountains and telescopes. Another photograph on my wall at home is of a young Indian girl—or is she a woman? Someone has written on the negative with a firm hand, "Pima Squaw," and she stands there with an olla of water resting on her head, her face closed to all who look upon it. She is frozen forever in the chemicals of photography at about the same time as the two young white women who are busy making fresh homes in a new country.

It is all so very far away from here; the harbor is thick with sea air, the mountain is just a word briefly existing in the smoky office air. The man I am talking to has lobbied Congress, browbeaten bureaucrats, coached his clients in the game of Washington, and he has just won. He has never seen the mountain. He calls for a file, his secretary enters, hips swinging in a tight skirt, the smile professional and the nails long and cared for.

The mountain? Ah, yes, the mountain. It will be safe, many careful plans will protect it, the animals will not suffer, knowledge will advance, the business will go on. It is out there somewhere, out there past the lacquered coyote skull, many days march past the bearskin rug. He must see it, in fact intends to do just that the next time he is out.

We talk for two hours; he is a blunt and friendly man. He knew he would win the mountain, knew it absolutely. No one, he tells me, will take small animals over telescopes that open up whole galaxies. I agree.

When he can swing it, he confides, he'd like to move out there with his wife and kids. The East, well, look at it. He likes it out there. He's figuring on a vacation soon. Where should he go in the desert? I give him some tips. He says, we gotta have a beer next time I am out there, okay?

I like the man. I hate what he is doing, what he is a part of. But then I do not feel too good about myself either. In the past we tended to remain silent while the ground that gives us life was murdered. Now we make studies of it before we kill it. Now we write stories protesting its death. And then we kill it, all of us, and share in the rewards of this act. And the desert, as one of the last places left for this taking, for this killing, is the place where today we find out who we are and what we are.

The desert is everywhere now, it is in millions of minds and they will not let it go. It is for sale, one can own it. Put it on a shelf and admire it. We rub our fingers across lacquered skulls. We no longer permit follies such as the wild wanderings of Coronado. We insist on permits, master plans, environmental impact statements. We favor fine photos of places without houses or people. We wish to belong. Strike roots.

We lack the capacity. Think of one hundred million years, fix the image firmly. It is not a possible thought for us. Try thinking of 800 years, centuries spent never stirring from one spot. That too is impossible. Consider spending one single year in one place and living with what that place offers up. This too is impossible. We are different from the things we admire in and of the desert and that is why we will never really belong here. It is because of our habits, our customs.

More than a century ago a man rode into the Sonoran Desert. He kept notes of what he saw and what happened. These notes tell our story, our endlessly repeating story. He wore gray through the Civil War and arrived on the Salt River in central Arizona with the first herd of Texas steers in January 1868. His name was Thomas Thompson Hunter. He gazed out on the valley and saw Pima women gathering mesquite near the river, two hundred fifty strung out in a long line with three-cornered baskets on their backs, long, slick sticks in their hands, and the look of a herd of cattle. When they had a load, they trotted home. On the nearby sand hills he saw a line of Pima warriors armed with bows and arrows, eyes sharp for Apaches.

Hunter moves his steers to the flats covered with the nutritious wild plant called alfileria in what is now downtown Phoenix. The cows are soon fat as butter. One day the stock shuns the rich grazing ground and he must drive them to their food. He finds another line of Pima women, naked to the waists but wearing beautiful necklaces. They work through the flat plucking caterpillars and eating them raw. The surplus they string with thread around their necks, the live worms wriggling on their breasts.

Twenty-eight years later, Hunter returns. The flat has become Phoenix. The warriors and women have become the government Indian school. They are forming up by platoon to parade through the city. There is a brass band followed by small boys in a drummer corps. The girls wear uniforms and move with the firm strides of an army. We hear the ticking of a different clock, a sense of time that insists that the desert accelerate, become something else, give way to our needs—and that is what always keeps us from the desert.

Visitors to the desert seem to follow two basic patterns. They either kill the desert, like Hunter, or the desert kills them. Perhaps a second story is in order.

This time the man is thirty-three years old, blond, and big-boned. He enters the Company of Jesus at age eighteen, studies, and then teaches college in Germany for seven years. He is ordained around his thirtieth year. At Cadiz, he sits waiting for a ship. Moorish pirates have driven everyone into port. After seventy-two days at sea, he lands at Vera Cruz. It is August 23, 1750.

He travels with other priests and they reach Guadalajara on December 19, 1750. They make up a party—ten missionaries (Father Baegert among them), twelve mule drivers and servants, unnumbered beasts. They drift slowly northward, dining at various towns along the way, eating dried beef, beans, and tortillas on the road. By March 9, 1751, they are on the banks of the Rio Yaqui, the southern edge of the huge, dry ground. Sometime in June or July of 1751, Father Henricus Ruhen, S. J., arrives at Sonoyta, the most western of Jesuit missions in the desert. He stays some weeks in the Indian village, then goes back to the larger mission at Tubutama.

On the night of November 21, 1751, he is at his post in Sonoyta. He lies in bed. It is a Sunday. Arrows come through the window and the priest is struck. He pulls himself up and creeps from the hut. He finds a tree, grabs hold of the trunk.

At dawn they find him clinging to the bark. A stone to his skull ends it. The people destroy the town. It is over here.

Six years later a visiting priest finds his bones and bloodstained skull and buries him. Father Henricus Ruhen, S. J., had lived in Sonoyta for about five months. Now he will sleep here forever. The visiting priest considers starting the mission up again, but it is not possible. He finds the local people "had conceived such an aversion for Christianity that on no account did they wish ever again to tolerate a missionary among them."

The stories to decorate the murder begin to flower. We have this need for stories to keep the facts at bay. A story claims that Father Ruhen was killed because he loved to ring the church bell, which in turn caused earthquakes. So the people break his arms and legs, throw him into the embrace of a cholla, and he suffers three days before dying. They burn the church, steal the altar and bell. The bell is, of course, solid gold. It is always so in stories.

The bell must be wrapped in blankets and buried in the sand to protect everyone from further earthquakes. The priest's rosary hangs on a tree for one hundred years or more. The altar, too, is menacing, according to the stories. It comes from the battle between I'itoi and a monster at Quitovac, a village near Sonoyta. The bones of the monster lay about the village, bones later men would claim were from a mammoth. The stone, well, the stone was the monster's heart.

In 1907 treasure hunters dig up the melted remains of the old mud church. They find large finger marks in the adobes, said to have come from the priest's giant hands. A body is found, the skeleton very large, the hair still clinging and blond.

The village itself drifts a mile to the west, tracking the channel alterations of the river. Now a cotton gin rumbles across from the dirt mound where the priest once slept on a November night. There is a small marker for his grave. And the sound of truck engines at idle as darkness falls down on the town.

If we try very hard there may be a third possible story for our kind here. First, we must learn to love something that does not love us, the desert. Secondly, we must learn to live in a place we can never stay. Third, we must accept the fact that we can change very little here, probably change nothing at all except for a very, very short run. On the coast of Sonora lives a tribe of people called the Seris and near them to the north a patch of boojums grow. They believe the plants are the remains of giants frozen in flight. And they are careful what they say around these plants because they believe that boojums can understand language. We find such a belief quaint and endearing and in our hearts we will have none of it.

That is why we call this living thing a boojum. It came to pass this way. In 1922 an Englishman named Godfrey Sykes crested a hill on the Sonoran coast and looked through a telescope and saw Idria columnaris Kellogg, saw el cirio. The first name is from the Linnean classification, the second is Spanish for a taper, since the plant resembles a tall candle. Sykes had read Lewis Carroll's The Hunting of the Snark and he remembered the reference to a strange thing that lived in a far-off, desolate land, a thing called a boojum. As he looked through his telescope, Sykes said, "Ho, ho, a boojum, definitely a boojum!"

The rains come when they will and things live or die because of this fact. No matter. The winds have little effect on the form, on that tower looming up into the sky. Ah, so very slender, sometimes as tall as a seven-story building, the flesh fat with moisture against the days of heat and burning soil. In the summer a refusal to drink, an absolute refusal. Pour the water on and the roots will not take it up, no, never, not at all. They rot rather than drink. The little branches that spike out from the flesh—touch it, touch it, please—these branches drop their leaves. But the roots seal and will not take up water, not a drop. There have been far too many dry years for any possible belief in summer. In the fall a contorting there, up there on the top, and then wands leap out, flowers open, and the roar of insects goes around and around for days. Almost a deafness comes from that sound. The air is filled with a soft, rich scent. Not a word, of course, never a sound. This is constantly said, a point absolutely insisted upon: that speech is not possible, nor hearing, nor knowing, nor moving. Or counting either. A year, eight hundred years, a million years, one hundred million years, what does it matter? The thing cannot count, cannot hear, speak, know. A thing, nothing but a thing. Heat, wind, light, dark, moisture, dryness, repeating again and again. All against the dumb thing.

Never, never leaving here. Staying, a deep staying, roots down into earth, roots plunging through hot soil to cool depths. This is known, can be measured, instruments spew forth numbers to convince one and all of this. See the chart, the rows of numbers? That is believable.

Belonging.

But they say the boojum has no feelings. Has no real identity. What to call the boojum? It? Them? He? She?

I? No, not I. That is not permitted. We have proofs of DNA, of different cell structures, of thumbs, cortexes, language—pay attention now, this matter of language is very important in making distinctions. We pride ourselves on language, we say it separates us from them. The mute, they can be treated with contempt. Much of the natural world is seen as a kind of Johnny Belinda, a tongue-tied thing ripe for rape. Don't you know?

But the I is very tempting. What if identity, feeling, actual consciousness is granted? What if our ears hear something on the wind, something saying, No one can speak for me. No one capable of speech can truly know what I say. I know this because . . . I cannot know.

And perhaps there is proof of this matter. Consider the pages in your hands, the images booming up rich with colors. Why do we fabricate these artifacts, these books of photographs and words about this other world we call nature? Because there are so many of us, billions of Homo sapiens, clawing at the window of life, our noses pressed against the glass. Us, crowded planet of us, all so anxious to get in, begging to get in. These books constitute our way of saying that we, too, belong. And we say it with the very evidence that proves our distance, that asserts our exclusion. We state our separateness with our lenses, film stocks, symbols, artifacts. We say we belong with a book spread out on our laps, the pages seducing us with songs made of colors.

Do you really believe that in the true beginning was the word?

Striking roots. No fear of the hot winds. A hundred million years.

What does it matter?

Come here. Now taste.

PALM CANYON, CALIFORNIA FAN PALMS IN KOFA MOUNTAINS. KOFA NATIONAL WILDLIFE REFUGE

GLOBEMALLOW (*Sphaeralcea coulteri*) AND TINY *Phacelia crenulata* ON THE CRACKED FLOODPLAIN OF THE TOHONO O'ODHAM INDIAN RESERVATION

NIGHT-BLOOMING CACTUS *(Peniocereus greggii)* BEFORE DAWN. TUCSON

BARREL CACTUS (*Ferocactus wislizenii*) DUSTED WITH NEW SNOW. SANTA CATALINA MOUNTAINS, CORONADO NATIONAL FOREST

GRANITE FORMATIONS, PONDEROSA PINE, AND POINT-LEAF MANZANITA (*Arctostaphylos pungens*). SANTA CATALINA MOUNTAINS, CORONADO NATIONAL FOREST

SNOW-DRAPED YUCCA (*Yucca schottii*) AND ARIZONA SYCAMORES IN BEAR CANYON. SANTA CATALINA MOUNTAINS, CORONADO NATIONAL FOREST

SUN RISES ON SAGUARO CACTUS (*Carnegiea gigantea*) FOREST BAJADA. TUCSON MOUNTAINS, SAGUARO NATIONAL MONUMENT

SNOW AT SUNRISE. SAGUARO NATIONAL MONUMENT, TUSCON MOUNTAINS UNIT

FINGER ROCK CANYON, SANTA CATALINA MOUNTAINS, CORONADO NATIONAL FOREST

PALO VERDE (*Parkinsonia aculeata*) WITH SEED POD AFTER RAIN. SAGUARO NATIONAL MONUMENT

HUMMINGBIRD TRUMPET (*Zauschneria californica*) AND BEGGAR'S TICK (*Bidens aurea*) IN BLOOM AMID GRANITE BOULDERS OF BEAR CREEK.
SANTA CATALINA MOUNTAINS, CORONADO NATIONAL FOREST

FLOWERS EMERGE FROM THE TIP OF A SAGUARO CACTUS LIMB. SAGUARO NATIONAL MONUMENT, TUCSON MOUNTAINS UNIT

SAGUARO CACTUS AT DAWN WITH FLOWERS EMERGING FROM ITS TWISTED LIMBS. SAGUARO NATIONAL MONUMENT, TUCSON MOUNTAINS UNIT

MORNING GLORIES (*Ipomoea leptotoma*) AND STAGHORN CHOLLA (*Opuntia versicolor*) COVER THE BOTTOM OF PIMA CANYON. SANTA CATALINA MOUNTAINS, CORONADO

NATIONAL FOREST

SIERRA TUSERAL, OCOTILLO, AND CHOLLA ON A BAJADA IN CABEZA PRIETA NATIONAL WILDLIFE REFUGE

A WATER-SCULPTED POOL KNOWN AS LITTLE WILD HORSE TANK ON THE WEST FLANK OF THE RINCON MOUNTAINS. SAGUARO NATIONAL MONUMENT,

RINCON MOUNTAINS UNIT

SABINO CANYON, SANTA CATALINA MOUNTAINS, CORONADO NATIONAL FOREST

BURNT PONDEROSA PINE WITH NEW GROWTH BRACKEN FERN (*Pteridium aquilinum*). SANTA CATALINA MOUNTAINS, CORONADO NATIONAL FOREST

GOLDEN COLUMBINE (*Aquilegia chrysantha*) AMID LADY FERNS (*Athyrium filix-femina*). SKY-ISLAND MOUNTAINS, SANTA CATALINA MOUNTAINS, CORONADO NATIONAL FOREST

TANGLED FISHHOOK CACTUS (*Mammillaria microcarpa*), TEDDY BEAR CHOLLA BUDS, AND TERMITE-RIDDEN, MUD-COVERED WOOD. CABEZA PRIETA WILDLIFE REFUGE

SAGUARO CACTUS, CLOAKFERNS (*Notholaena aurea*) AND AGAVE. ESPERERO CANYON, SANTA CATALINA MOUNTAINS. CORONADO NATIONAL FOREST

SEVEN FALLS IN BEAR CANYON ROARS WITH WINTER STORM RUNOFF. SANTA CATALINA MOUNTAINS, CORONADO NATIONAL FOREST

SPRING RUNOFF IN A SAGUARO CACTUS FOREST BAJADA. SANTA CATALINA MOUNTAINS, CORONADO NATIONAL FOREST

A MONSOON POURS RAIN ON A FOREST OF SAGUARO CACTI. SAGUARO NATIONAL MONUMENT, TUCSON MOUNTAINS UNIT

SAGUARO CACTUS SKELETAL RIBS WITH ARMS STILL IN PLACE. SAGUARO NATIONAL MONUMENT, TUSCON MOUNTAINS UNIT

A FULL MOON RISES OVER SAGUARO CACTI. TUCSON MOUNTAINS, SAGUARO NATIONAL MONUMENT

A PAIR OF SAGUARO CACTI. SAGUARO NATIONAL MONUMENT, TUCSON MOUNTAINS UNIT

MONSOON CLOUDS FILL THE SKY NEAR THE ANTELOPE HILLS. CABEZA PRIETA NATIONAL WILDLIFE REFUGE

SAGUARO CACTI LINE AN ARROYO AMID CREOSOTE BUSH (*Larrea tridentata*) FLAT NEAR THE MEXICAN BORDER. CABEZA PRIETA NATIONAL WILDLIFE REFUGE

FALL FOLIAGE OF BIGTOOTH MAPLE, SYCAMORE, AND VELVET ASH (*Fraxinus velutina*). RATTLESNAKE CANYON, GALIURO MOUNTAINS, CORONADO NATIONAL FOREST

PASSIFLORA VINES (*Passiflora mexicana*) AND NETLEAF HACKBERRY (*Celtis reticulata*) IN HOT SPRINGS CANYON AT
THE MULESHOE RANCH NATURE CONSERVANCY PRESERVE. GALIURO MOUNTAINS

COTTONWOOD (*Populus fremontii*) WITH SAGUARO CACTUS. ARAVAIPA CREEK, ARAVAIPA CANYON WILDERNESS

RIME-COVERED PONDEROSA PINE (*Pinus ponderosa*) UNDER A LIFTING WINTER STORM. MOUNT WRIGHTSON, SANTA RITA MOUNTAINS, CORONADO NATIONAL FOREST

VIRGUS CANYON CONFLUENCE WITH ARAVAIPA CREEK. SYCAMORE (*Platanus wrightii*) LEAVES COVERING THE STREAM'S POOLS WITH FALL COLOR. ARAVAIPA CANYON

GOLDEN COLUMBINE AND SCARLET MONKEY FLOWERS (*Mimulus cardinalus*) IN THE MULESHOE RANCH NATURE CONSERVANCY PRESERVE.
BASS CANYON, GALIURO MOUNTAINS

SYCAMORE LEAVES AND WATERCRESS (*Nasturtium officinale*) LINE THE BANKS OF TURKEY CREEK. GALIURO MOUNTAINS

RATTLESNAKE CREEK REFLECTS BIGTOOTH MAPLE (*Acer grandidentatum*) LEAVES AND THE CANYON WALL. GALIURO MOUNTAINS, CORONADO NATIONAL FOREST

MEXICAN POPPIES (*Eschscholzia californica* subspecies *mexicana*) AMID FALLEN SKELETAL RIBS OF A SAGUARO CACTUS. PICACHO PEAK STATE PARK

MEXICAN POPPY AMID DECAYING SAGUARO CACTUS. PICACHO STATE PARK

SAGUARO CACTUS SKELETON WITH THE SIERRA ANCHAS MOUNTAINS IN THE BACKGROUND AT SUNSET.

MAZATZAL MOUNTAINS, SYCAMORE CREEK, TONTO NATIONAL FOREST

SAGUARO CACTUS AMID IRONWOOD (*Olneya tesota*) AND FOOTHILL PALO VERDE (*Cercidium microphyllum*). SUPERSTITION MOUNTAINS, TONTO NATIONAL FOREST

IN A SONORAN-MOHAVE TRANSITION ZONE IN NORTHWEST ARIZONA A JOSHUA TREE (*Yucca brevifolia*) STANDS SILHOUETTED. JOSHUA FOREST PARKWAY

THE DRY LAKE BED OF WILLCOX PLAYA LIES FLOODED AFTER RAIN. IN THE BACKGROUND ARE THE DOS CABEZAS AND CHIRICAHUA MOUNTAINS. THE AREA LIES BETWEEN
THE SONORAN AND CHIHUAHUAN DESERTS

OCOTILLO AND WHITE BRITTLEBUSH (*Encelia farinosa*) AMID VOLCANIC ROCK. BATES MOUNTAINS, ORGAN PIPE CACTUS NATIONAL MONUMENT

ORGANPIPE CACTUS AND TEDDY BEAR CHOLLA LINE THE RIDGES IN FRONT OF THE AJO MOUNTAINS.

ORGAN PIPE CACTUS NATIONAL MONUMENT

ELEPHANT HEAD OF THE SANTA RITA MOUNTAINS RISES OVER THE SANTA CRUZ VALLEY AND A LINE OF MESQUITE TREES *(Prosopis velutina)*. CORONADO NATIONAL FOREST

A LINE OF SAGUARO CACTI AT SUNSET. SAN PEDRO VALLEY, EAST OF TUCSON

ORGANPIPE CACTUS AT SUNSET. ORGAN PIPE CACTUS NATIONAL MONUMENT

TEDDY BEAR CHOLLA IN KOFA QUEEN CANYON. KOFA NATIONAL WILDLIFE REFUGE

DESERT BEING CLEARED TO PRODUCE ALFALFA FOR CATTLE. NEAR SANTA ANA, SONORA, MEXICO

SIX

He saw it first from the open door of a boxcar in 1944, when he was seventeen years old. He saw it last from the floor of his shack in the very early morning hours of March 14, 1989, when he was sixty-two years old and blood gushed willy-nilly out the broken-down veins of his body and his flesh went cold. His name was Edward Abbey. He was my friend and this is no help in explaining either him or the ground that claimed him once and for all. The voice, it was very low and, oddly enough, soft. The words were precise, the manner at first low-key, but the face almost intense, a small smile screening a volcano of anger. He thought no one should be here, he thought he should not be here. He stops his words, looks at me in the noisy cafe and asks if I noticed that woman across the room eating a hamburger, the juice from the meat on her lips. Life is never a mess, but it is always messy, like a tidal pool.

He wrote about twenty books, but his reputation has remained largely regional, a legend locked into the small pockets of human beings in the largely empty ground we call the West, and more especially the Southwest. This fact did not sit well with him but he was helpless to remedy it because he was a captive of a place he said was empty of meaning and unfit to live in. He kept claiming he would change, that he would write no more about this ground, the rocks, the heat, the emptiness, that he had had his say. And I think he meant it, and truly he did write of other things. But he could not let it go.

He married often, divorced often, preached zero population growth, and left five children in his wake. Sometimes he drank too much, sometimes he lost his temper and said and wrote hard things, ugly things. He would say that people who suffer from AIDS should be left in the desert to die. He would say that Mexican immigration must be stopped because Hispanic culture hates the earth, hates nature, and will bring its poison north and ruin us. At other times he played the recorder sitting on a rock in the middle of nowhere, and seemed as benign as a spring flower. Once he was late for lunch and apologized, and when we went out later to the parking lot the front of his truck was caved in. He explained he had had a head-on collision en route. Later he fastened a plastic flower to the busted prow of his old machine.

Mainly, he said whatever he had to say better than anyone else. He was as wily as a coyote, and as deadly as a snake. The wit of the man was a pleasure, the venom alarming. Fortunately there were no big moments in our friendship to ruin its calm. But sometimes I worry that he may have managed to poison me with a fatal dose of, well, ethics.

I remember going one night to an environmental rally down at El Rio Neighborhood Center. The evening chugged along with the expected dose of environmental pep talks, sensitive poetry readings, and we-ain't-going-to-take-this-anymore war cries. The audience was

SPRAY-PAINTED GRANITE BOULDERS NEAR JOSHUA TREE NATIONAL MONUMENT, CALIFORNIA wall-to-wall waffle stompers and plaid flannel shirts, the women had long hair and no makeup. Then Abbey's turn came and he pulled some pages out of his pocket and started reading a long, shaggy-dog story about his earlier days in Albuquerque, about roaring down the road with a pal, tossing beer cans out the window and firing a pistol wildly into the countryside. I could feel the crowd get edgy. Abbey droned on seemingly oblivious, and his text somehow segued into the charms and joys of various sorority girls encountered in those college adventures. I sensed a sullen steam begin to rise up off the audience. Suddenly he was finished and the evening promptly returned to environmental proprieties.

I thought: well, why pander?

Then there was the time he called me up and asked if I'd be interested in going to Mexico City. Architectural Digest had commissioned him to assess some fancy mansion there designed by a leading architect, and there were nice, crisp dollars to finance a reconnaissance. I thought, what the hell. A few weeks later, the trip was off. They'd sent him pictures of the house and he couldn't stand the way it looked. He told me he couldn't write about an obscene thing like that.

I thought: well, don't just do it for the money.

A month or so before he died, he was showing me his toy, an old red Cadillac convertible. I said, "Christ, Ed, you've got no shame." And then he stopped living. So I'm left with: You don't pander; you don't roll over for money; and you drive any damn thing you want.

And these words he left on paper.

THE DESERT IS ALSO A-TONAL, CRUEL, CLEAR, INHUMAN, NEITHER ROMANTIC NOR CLASSICAL, MOTIONLESS AND EMOTIONLESS, AT ONE AND THE SAME TIME—ANOTHER PARADOX—BOTH AGONIZED AND DEEPLY STILL. LIKE DEATH? PERHAPS.[23]

He kept making this same point over and over: there is nothing really out there, it is just this blank we like to write our minds on. "But," he noted in explaining his attraction to the place with nothing, "there was nothing out there. Nothing at all. Nothing but desert. Nothing but the silent world. That's why." [24]

But the silent world needs its friends. One day recently I came out of the Sierra Madre on foot down in Sonora and found a guy about sixty sitting by his VW camper having a cold beer. So I joined him. He said he'd run around the West all his life, and way back in the early 1950s he went to school up in Albuquerque with a guy named Ed Abbey, a writer guy. They started taking out billboards at night, first chopping them down, then getting chain saws, and finally, when the companies went to steel posts set in concrete, using dynamite. There are many such tales, and they accomplish two things: they've made Abbey a cult, and they scare the hell out of many other people. I suspect for Abbey they just happened. I do not understand why the stories frighten anyone who looks and sees what is happening.

"I don't believe," he once wrote with the fine feeling of a son of Appalachia, "in doing work I don't want to do in order to live the way I don't want to live." [25]

He had a gut hatred of modern industrialism, of a machine culture that creates machine people to tend to its needs. He could hardly write a page, comic or tragic, without this feeling lashing out: "Which was the worthier technological achievement, the moon landing or the invention of bread? The bake oven or the nuclear reactor? Only a fool would hesitate to answer."

He was careful of his denims and old shirts, careful of his hair and beard, more than careful of his writing. I am out at the house, his old black dog is dying of Valley fever, a local fungal plague of man and beast, and he jokes and complains of having to dose the dog with medicine and how much the medicine costs him and that he is a fool to persist in this indulgence. And then this fat novel comes out, The Fool's Progress: An Honest Novel, and the damn dog and the damn medicine and the damn complaint is there. Except for the joke. When he wrote the book he was dying, but forgot to tell anyone and the dog, well, the dog outlived him. A last cut of the cards, aces wild.

Abbey was a gambler and the desert was his last trick. The wolf, he made a raid and then retreated. Cabeza de Vaca, he paid a blood price most of us cannot even imagine, was conquered by a world, came out naked and nearer to some kind of god. The ants, those tiny, insignificant things that will outlast us all—they avoid, they go deep into the earth, they know how to belong. Coronado, he is our true nature, the part of us that comes only to take, and flees when loot is not freely offered. The boojum, with that arrogant patience and the centuries of time, we cannot know and barely can tolerate.

But Abbey, he is within our reach. Besides, he has not marched that far out in front of us. He hates our cities, as do we all, and dreams of their ruin in book after book. He writes a novel called The Monkey Wrench Gang, which explores the destruction of Glen Canyon Dam. He writes a novel entitled Good News, which explores the American Southwest after the final collapse. And yet he lives in towns and cities, always publishing fictitious addresses. He takes hikes here and there and then carefully disguises the geography so that we cannot find out exactly where he has been. He keeps telling us we do not belong here, that he does not belong here. And he won't leave.

He is our tongue, saying things we cannot bring ourselves to say. He is our sins written large and does not deny this fact. After all the man drank too much, chased women, drove cars, threw trash out the windows, lived in a house not a wigwam, consumed things, made noise at times. But he felt in his bones what we feel. They predict now that world population will peak at eleven billion in the year 2150. They predict now that the last tropical tree will be felled in the year 2135. We have almost lost the will to even argue with these predictions. We feel their truths in our bones. So we turn to the casino, to the game, to the gambling we have always known and loved. We find it is easier that way. [26]

The game is almost over and this is the last deal in one of the last places left. That is why it still persists—our ancestors couldn't figure out how to rape it. There they are cutting the cards, pick one up, put a house on it, build a hideaway, make it a park with nice paved roads, post little signs telling us things about nature we will never remember. Bury toxic wastes perhaps, test odd weapons—no one will notice here. Run strange machines, 4 x 4s, motorcycles, dune buggies, don't worry, for God's sake, there is nothing out there but cactus and snakes and scorpions. Build a gallery, hang large color photographs on the wall, sit there, right over there on that very long couch, sip a cold drink—we deserve that drink—and enjoy the sunset trapped inside the frame on the wall, the colors rich and intense thanks to that smear of chemicals. Write a book explaining a sensitive reaction to this dry ecosystem.

Keep demanding more cards, they'll never run out of cards, the house guarantees endless decks. If we get worried, we can commission more studies, statements that track impacts, perhaps set up little reserves where we can watch birds, or feel the great beauty of the stone in the shifting light. By all means, be reasonable, never use violence, it is wrong; never destroy property, it is wrong. Never side with other forms of life—such treason cannot and will not be forgiven.

If things get too bad, try whiskey. If that is not enough, try pills. If that is not sufficient, consider coke. Do not hesitate to ask for other substances, they will be provided. Do not feel bad about such acts—God, we must not feel bad—everyone in this place needs drugs to drown out the silence.

Be advised: stay in the casino. Anyone leaving the premises—well, the management cannot be held responsible if we commit such an act. And we could die out there, we really could. It is very hot, there is little water, the plants have claws that tear at our flesh, the vipers have poison, the insects are fierce. Besides, there is no need to wander, the casino keeps expanding, adding more rooms, more parking. Look, a mirror in the ceiling. We must be in heaven.

Ed, he just wouldn't listen. I talked to him one Wednesday night and he sounded fine. Thursday he went on the table. Friday his wife said he would be all right. Sunday—or was it Monday?—he looked up from his hospital bed, all those tubes connecting him to

CENTRAL ARIZONA PROJECT, NEAR SCOTTSDALE, ARIZONA

machines and jugs and juices that dripped into his veins, and he said to his wife, "I'm leaving. Are you coming with me?" He sat up all night under a tree waiting to die. The blood kept flowing out of him. But he failed, he failed at this simple task. He always was a kind of half-assed hillbilly at heart. They returned to the shack down by the wash where he wrote and listened to classical music and smoked bad cigars. He died on the floor just after dawn.

And then he pulled one more trick. They packed him in a sleeping bag, laid on some ice, and roared off into the white light. A long way off, they pulled over, dragged the body out there—way out there, no music now, no soft light, no air-conditioning, no more cards— and dug a hole and laid him in it. He lied to us, just as we all lie to us. He said there is nothing out there. A lie. He said we couldn't stay. And now he's checked into the place for what looks to be eternity.

But he understood the game. He saw through the phony house rules about progress, development, taking care of the environment, having our desert and factories too. He knew the only thing of value to be found here was the barest glimmer of an understanding about just what the word place might mean. Something that we do not conquer, something that does not care about us, something that might fill the emptiness that has driven us for so very long. Some place where we might belong even though we cannot stay except as a gesture. And the place has not suffered for this act. The silence is still there, the white glare, the songs of coyotes in the night, the track of the snake across the sand, the trail of ants carrying little bits of leaves.

We seem to want a world where there is a master plan and this plan states that our behavior will not be punished, our appetites will not be curbed, our present will not determine our future. We will be exempt from death, from hunger, from pain, from everything but love. And love will not be earned but freely given like that of a parent to a child. We say that such a world is our due, is our right, is part of the master plan. We say this to our politicians, to our friends, to our gods, to our dreams. But we do not go to the desert and say this, no, not there. Out on the hot ground we fall silent because there finally we know what we have always denied, though not a word is said to explain this fact to us. The desert will not sustain our lies but instead offers a taste of life. And out on the ground there is no master and there is no plan but there is death and hunger and pain. Because, as we always suspected, the desert does not care. And finally, love becomes a possibility.

We already know more than we will ever understand.

We already understand more than we will ever need in order to take action.

We are ready now.

We must do it.

Or . . . we will kill it.

We have been at its throat so very, very long.

PRESS THE PEDAL TO THE FLOOR. THE BIG BRUTE MOTOR WILL GRUMBLE LIKE A LION, OLD, TIRED, HESITATING, THEN CATCH FIRE AND ROAR, EIGHT-HEARTED IN ITS BLOCK OF IRON, DRIVING ONWARD, WESTWARD ALWAYS, INTO THE SUN.[27]

DUMPING NEAR MULEGE, BAJA CALIFORNIA SUR

NOTES

1   *Anyone interested in the odyssey of the Mexican wolf in the last century should consult: David E. Brown,* THE WOLF IN THE SOUTHWEST: THE MAKING OF AN ENDANGERED SPECIES. *Tucson: University of Arizona Press, 1983; James C. Bednarz,* THE MEXICAN WOLF: BIOLOGY, HISTORY, AND PROSPECTS FOR REESTABLISHMENT IN NEW MEXICO, *U.S. Fish and Wildlife Service, Endangered Species Report 18, Albuquerque, New Mexico, 1988; Bednarz,* AN EVALUATION OF THE ECOLOGICAL POTENTIAL OF WHITE SANDS MISSILE RANGE TO SUPPORT A REINTRODUCED POPULATION OF MEXICAN WOLVES, *U.S. Fish and Wildlife Service Endangered Species Report 19, Albuquerque, New Mexico, 1989.*

2   *E. O. Wilson, ed.,* BIODIVERSITY. *Washington, D.C.: National Academy Press, 1988. See particularly the essays by Wilson, Paul R. Ehrlich, and Norman Myers.*

3   *The image is from James E. Lovelock, author of the provocative Gaia theory, in Wilson,* BIODIVERSITY.

4   *Cyclone Covey, trans and ed.,* ADVENTURES IN THE UNKNOWN INTERIOR OF AMERICA. *Albuquerque: University of New Mexico Press, 1990 [1961], 91.*

5   *Quoted in Morris Bishop,* THE ODYSSEY OF CABEZA DE VACA., *New York, The Century Company, 1933, 189.*

6   *Covey,* ADVENTURES IN THE UNKNOWN INTERIOR OF AMERICA, *67.*

7   *There is one interesting exception, Haniel Long's* INTERLINEAR TO CABEZA DE VACA, *a tiny volume of thirty-seven pages first published in the late thirties and then reissued during the Second World War as* THE POWER WITHIN US *(New York: Duell, Sloan and Pearce, 1944), where it went through four editions. Long presumed to write what Cabeza de Vaca would have said had the times permitted such thoughts. "But only," his Cabeza de Vaca notes, "when at last relaxed, could I see the possibilities of a life in which to be deprived of Europe was not to be deprived of too much." It is a book well worth reading. But perhaps it will require another world war to return it to favor.*

8   *Covey,* ADVENTURES IN THE UNKNOWN INTERIOR OF AMERICA, *120.*

9   *Ibid.*

10   *Ibid.*

11   *Quoted in Kirkpatrick Sale,* THE CONQUEST OF PARADISE: CHRISTOPHER COLUMBUS AND THE COLUMBIAN LEGACY. *New York: Alfred A. Knopf, 1990, 104. Sale himself says, "One could argue that all cultures, to some degree, 'war against' their environment . . . Is there something about the attitudes and practices of Europe that make it so different? The answer would seem to be yes. . . . [N]owhere else was the essential reverence for nature seriously challenged, nowhere did there emerge the idea that human achievement and material betterment were to be won by* OPPOSING *nature, nowhere any equivalent to that frenzy and destruction that we find on the Western record." Ibid., 88.*

12   *Covey,* ADVENTURES IN THE UNKNOWN INTERIOR OF AMERICA, *122.*

13   *Ibid.*

14   *Ibid.*

15   *William Woodruff,* IMPACT OF WESTERN MAN. *New York: St. Martin's Press, 1967, 16.*

16   *Perhaps the most touching example of this slaughter was recorded by the great traveler, naturalist, and thinker Alexander von Humboldt on his visit to South America at the beginning of the nineteenth century. He found in one instance that the sole surviving speaker of one tribal language was a parrot he came upon in a village.*

17   *The following account and the information on Atta Mexicana are taken from William Morton Wheeler,* THE FUNGUS-GROWING ANTS OF NORTH AMERICA. *New York: Dover Publications, Inc., 1973. This is a reprint of "The Fungus Growing Ants of North America," Article XXXI of the* BULLETIN OF THE AMERICAN MUSEUM OF NATURAL HISTORY, *Vol. XXIII, 1907: 669–807.*

18   *For those weary of the same old magazines scattered about on the coffee table, I heartily recommend "Backyard BUGwatching," Sonoran Arthropod Studies, Inc., P. O. Box 56254, Tucson, Arizona, 85703. It comes with a twenty-dollar membership in SASI. Where else are you going to find that article about bugs featured on postage stamps?*

19   *Probably the best book ever written on another life form is Bert Hölldobler and Edward O. Wilson,* THE ANTS. *Cambridge, Mass.: The Belknap Press of Harvard University Press, 1990. See pages 596–608 for information on fungus-growing ants.*

20   *The following account of Coronado's expedition and the events leading up to it is based on George P. Hammond and Agapito Rey, eds.,* NARRATIVES OF THE CORONADO EXPEDITION OF 1540–1542. *(Albuquerque: University of New Mexico Press, 1940), and particularly on the history of the march contained therein by an actual member of the expedition, Pedro de Castañeda de Nájera, a singularly moving document.*

21   *The diary, 194 pages of handwriting entitled* ARIZONA MINES, GADSDEN PURCHASE, GEORGE KIPPEN, *1854, San Francisco, Calif., is kept in the vault of the Arizona State Archives in Phoenix. Kippen died in 1869.*

22   *Information on the climate of the Baja portion of the Sonoran Desert comes from Robert R. Humphrey,* THE BOOJUM AND ITS HOME. *Tucson: University of Arizona Press, 1974.*

23   *Edward Abbey,* DESERT SOLITAIRE. *Tucson: University of Arizona Press, 1988 [1968], 241.*

24   *Edward Abbey,* THE JOURNEY HOME: SOME WORDS IN DEFENSE OF THE AMERICAN WEST. *New York: E.P. Dutton, 1977, 22.*

25   *Edward Abbey,* THE FOOL'S PROGRESS: AN HONEST NOVEL. *New York: Avon Books, 1990 [1988].*

26   *Wilson,* BIODIVERSITY, *10.*

27   *Abbey,* THE FOOL'S PROGRESS: AN HONEST NOVEL. *A truly contradictory book, which is one reason among many that Abbey called it an honest novel of a fool's progress.*

The Story of Little Quack

To young writers of Brandon School Division #40
B.G. & K.M.D.

Kids Can Press Ltd. acknowledges with appreciation the assistance of the Canada Council and the Ontario Arts Council in the production of this book.

Canadian Cataloguing in Publication Data

Gibson, Betty
The story of little quack

ISBN 0-921103-97-2 (bound) ISBN 1-55074-063-6 (pbk.)

I. Denton, Kady MacDonald. II. Title.
PS8563.I28S84   1990   jC813'.54   C89-090564-9
PZ7.G526Sc   1990

PA 91 0 9 8 7 6 5 4 3

Kids Can Press Ltd.,
585½ Bloor Street West,
Toronto, Ontario, Canada, M6G 1K5.

Book design by N.R. Jackson
Printed and bound in Hong Kong

THE STORY of LITTLE QUACK

WRITTEN BY BETTY GIBSON

ILLUSTRATED BY KADY MacDONALD DENTON

Kids Can Press Ltd.,
Toronto

Jackie lived on a farm. He had a hen called Cluck and a dog named Woof. He had Buck the pony and a clumsy calf called Buttercup. But Jackie was lonesome.

Cluck was always busy laying eggs. Woof followed Jackie's father wherever he went. Buck galloped to the pasture every day and Buttercup ran off with the other cows. No one stayed to play with Jackie.

One day, Jackie's mother brought him a duck.
"I'll call her Little Quack," said Jackie.
Little Quack was the perfect pet. She had plenty
of time to play.

Every morning, when Jackie let the hens out into the yard, Little Quack followed him.

Every evening, when Jackie went to get the cows,
Little Quack came, too. When Jackie went paddling in
the pond, Little Quack swam beside him.

Jackie wasn't lonely anymore.
"You are my very best friend," said Jackie.

One day, Jackie and Little Quack went exploring.
Jackie took her to the barn to see the kittens and
piglets and lambs. He let her see Cluck and her yellow chicks.

Then they went to the pasture.

Jackie showed Little Quack where the lark had built her home. He showed her the robin's nest on the maple branch, and the hollow tree where a squirrel had a family.

They met Buttercup and Woof, but neither of them paid attention to Little Quack.

One morning, Jackie couldn't find Little Quack.
His mother helped him search, but together they could
not find Little Quack.

Jackie was very sad.

"I wonder if she went over the brook to Apple Hill Farm," said Jackie's father. "They have ducks there. Maybe Little Quack heard them when you walked with her in the pasture. Perhaps she is lonely."

"She couldn't be lonely," said Jackie. "I'm her friend and I always play with her."

"Yes, but she might be lonely for other ducks just as you are sometimes lonely for other children."

Jackie and his father went to Apple Hill Farm.
And there she was!

Little Quack waddled over to Jackie and followed
him home.

Every morning Little Quack waited for Jackie on
the doorstep. Every day Jackie and Little Quack
worked and played together.

One day, Little Quack disappeared again. This time she was not at Apple Hill Farm.

Jackie tried to play with the other animals. But Woof ran off after the tractor. Cluck had her chicks to guard and Buttercup had grown too big to play.

A dozen times a day Jackie said, "Little Quack,
I wish you'd come home."
But a month went by and Jackie gave up hoping
she would return.

One day, Jackie went to the far end of the pasture. He saw the lark's nest and chased a butterfly. He threw some corn to the gophers. Buttercup licked Jackie's hand and wandered off again. Buck tried to nibble Jackie's shirt and then ran away on his wobbly legs.

"I wish I had my duck," said Jackie.
Then he came to the brook.

There was Little Quack. And swimming with her were ten fluffy ducklings.

Little Quack came out of the water. Jackie fed
Little Quack some corn. The ducklings came out, too.
"Quack, quack, quack," they said.

How would he get Little Quack and her family to
the barnyard? He picked up the damp little ducklings
and carried them home in his old felt hat.

"Look!" called Jackie to his mother. "I found Little
Quack, and she has babies!"

"Little Quack won't be lonely now," said Jackie's mother.

"I won't be lonely either," Jackie said, filling the old tub with water. "Now I have Little Quack and her quacklings."

And the ducks swam round and round.